**Understanding
World History**

# Ancient
# Rome

**Hal Marcovitz**

**Bruno Leone
Series Consultant**

ReferencePoint
Press®

San Diego, CA

© 2012 ReferencePoint Press, Inc.
Printed in the United States

**For more information, contact:**
ReferencePoint Press, Inc.
PO Box 27779
San Diego, CA 92198
www.ReferencePointPress.com

LIBRARY OF CONGRESS CATALOGING-IN-PUBLICATION DATA

Marcovitz, Hal.
  Ancient Rome / Hal Marcovitz.
     p. cm. — (Understanding world history series)
  Includes bibliographical references and index.
  ISBN-13: 978-1-60152-186-6 (hardback)
  ISBN-10: 1-60152-186-3 (hardback)
  1. Rome—History—Juvenile literature. 2. Rome—Civilization—Juvenile literature. I. Title.
  DG209.M368 2012
  937—dc22
                                                                                    2010053305

# Contents

# Foreword

**W**hen the Puritans first emigrated from England to America in 1630, they believed that their journey was blessed by a covenant between themselves and God. By the terms of that covenant they agreed to establish a community in the New World dedicated to what they believed was the true Christian faith. God, in turn, would reward their fidelity by making certain that they and their descendants would always experience his protection and enjoy material prosperity. Moreover, the Lord guaranteed that their land would be seen as a shining beacon—or in their words, a "city upon a hill,"—which the rest of the world would view with admiration and respect. By embracing this notion that God could and would shower his favor and special blessings upon them, the Puritans were adopting the providential philosophy of history—meaning that history is the unfolding of a plan established or guided by a higher intelligence.

The concept of intercession by a divine power is only one of many explanations of the driving forces of world history. Historians and philosophers alike have subscribed to numerous other ideas. For example, the ancient Greeks and Romans argued that history is cyclical. Nations and civilizations, according to these ancients of the Western world, rise and fall in unpredictable cycles; the only certainty is that these cycles will persist throughout an endless future. The German historian Oswald Spengler (1880–1936) echoed the ancients to some degree in his controversial study *The Decline of the West*. Spengler asserted that all civilizations inevitably pass through stages comparable to the life span of a person: childhood, youth, adulthood, old age, and, eventually, death. As the title of his work implies, Western civilization is currently entering its final stage.

Joining those who see purpose and direction in history are thinkers who completely reject the idea of meaning or certainty. Rather, they reason that since there are far too many random and unseen factors at work on the earth, historians would be unwise to endorse historical predictability of any type. Warfare (both nuclear and conventional), plagues, earthquakes, tsunamis, meteor showers, and other catastrophic world-changing events have loomed large throughout history and prehistory. In his essay "A Free Man's Worship," philosopher and mathematician Bertrand Russell (1872–1970) supported this argument, which many refer to as the nihilist or chaos theory of history. According to Russell, history follows no preordained path. Rather, the earth itself and all life on earth resulted from, as Russell describes it, an "accidental collocation of atoms." Based on this premise, he pessimistically concluded that all human achievement will eventually be "buried beneath the debris of a universe in ruins."

Whether history does or does not have an underlying purpose, historians, journalists, and countless others have nonetheless left behind a record of human activity tracing back nearly 6,000 years. From the dawn of the great ancient Near Eastern civilizations of Mesopotamia and Egypt to the modern economic and military behemoths China and the United States, humanity's deeds and misdeeds have been and continue to be monitored and recorded. The distinguished British scholar Arnold Toynbee (1889–1975), in his widely acclaimed 12-volume work entitled *A Study of History,* studied 21 different civilizations that have passed through history's pages. He noted with certainty that others would follow.

In the final analysis, the academic and journalistic worlds mostly regard history as a record and explanation of past events. From a more practical perspective, history represents a sequence of building blocks—cultural, technological, military, and political—ready to be utilized and enhanced or maligned and perverted by the present. What that means is that all societies—whether advanced civilizations or preliterate tribal cultures—leave a legacy for succeeding generations to either embrace or disregard.

Recognizing the richness and fullness of history, the ReferencePoint Press Understanding World History series fosters an evaluation and interpretation of history and its influence on later generations. Each volume in the series approaches its subject chronologically and topically, with specific focus on nations, periods, or pivotal events. Primary and secondary source quotations are included, along with complete source notes and suggestions for further research.

Moreover, the series reflects the truism that the key to understanding the present frequently lies in the past. With that in mind, each series title concludes with a legacy chapter that highlights the bonds between past and present and, more important, demonstrates that world history is a continuum of peoples and ideas, sometimes hidden but there nonetheless, waiting to be discovered by those who choose to look.

# Important Events in Ancient Rome

**396 BC**
The Roman army lays siege to the city of Veii, conquering the last Etruscan stronghold in Italy. Rome is now master of the Italian Peninsula.

**753 BC**
Romulus—or a similar warrior—leads his followers to a bend in the Tiber River in central Italy, establishing a settlement that will grow into the city of Rome.

**509 BC**
The Etruscan king Tarquinius Superbus is ousted during a rebellion sparked by the rape of an aristocrat's wife by the king's son. After Tarquinius leaves the throne, the Roman Senate declares that Rome will be a *res publica*—a republic.

650 BC     500     350     200

**616 BC**
Lucius Tarquinius Priscus, the first of the Etruscan kings, seizes power in Rome. Priscus begins building the Roman Forum and other important buildings of Rome's ancient era.

**494 BC**
Ordinary Romans, or plebeians, stage the First Plebeian Secession, forcing the Senate to create the position of tribune, an officeholder who represents the interests of the common people.

**387 BC**
Rome suffers its first major defeat when Gallic invaders under Brennus rout the Roman army and sack the city.

**264 BC**
Rome sparks the first Punic War, ousting the Carthaginians from the island of Sicily while extracting a massive penalty from the North African city-state of Carthage.

**ca. 450 BC**
Another step toward democracy is achieved when the Roman Senate adopts the Twelve Tables, a set of laws—etched in stone—that requires obedience from all Roman citizens.

**218 BC**
The Second Punic War is waged by the Carthaginians under their military leader Hannibal. Despite early victories that threaten Rome, Hannibal is eventually defeated, and Carthage is sacked by the Romans.

**AD 80**

Construction of the Colosseum is completed. The magnificent amphitheater seats more than 50,000 spectators, who attend gladiatorial contests and other games 100 days or more a year.

**149 BC**

A brief Third Punic War is waged against the Carthaginians. Aided by Numidian tribespeople in North Africa, Rome wipes out the final remnants of Carthaginian society.

**AD 101**

Roman Emperor Trajan leads a conquering army against Dacia in central Europe. After conquering Dacia, the territory assumes the name Romania, or land of the Romans. It will be the last major conquest achieved by a Roman army.

**27 BC**

The Senate grants Octavius unlimited authority. He takes the name Augustus, becoming Rome's first emperor.

**AD 410**

Visigoth leader Alaric sacks Rome, encountering little resistance from the Roman army or the city's inhabitants.

**49 BC**

Caesar returns to Rome but ignores the Senate's orders to disband his army. Instead, he seizes power as dictator.

**150    100    50    50 AD    250    450**

**58 BC**

Roman general Gaius Julius Caesar avenges the Gallic sacking of Rome by conquering much of Gaul.

**AD 64**

Fire sweeps through Rome. Looking for a scapegoat, Emperor Nero accuses a small religious sect, the Christians, of setting the blaze, touching off a long era of Christian persecution in Rome.

**AD 293**

Emperor Diocletian splits the empire into four sections, each administered by a caesar. As one of the four rulers, Diocletian moves his capital away from Rome to a city in present-day Turkey.

**AD 476**

The final western Roman emperor, a teenager named Romulus, ascends to the throne of what remains of the empire. He reigns for just a few months, then steps down as a German monarch, Odoacer, declares himself king of Italy.

**44 BC**

Caesar is assassinated by patricians who feel he is growing too powerful. His death sparks a long civil war in which his adopted son, Octavius, emerges as the new leader of Rome.

# The Defining Characteristics of Ancient Rome

Two thousand years ago, Rome was the center of the civilized world and the most powerful city-state in existence. At its height the Roman Empire stretched from Scotland to Spain to Syria. The Roman army was well-trained, powerful, and merciless. The Roman navy was the master of the Mediterranean Sea. To be a Roman meant enjoying the benefits of citizenship in a civilization on the cutting edge of progress in philosophy and literature as well as the arts and sciences.

But Rome was hardly a utopian society. A very small minority of Romans, the patricians, controlled the empire's vast wealth. For most everyone else—the ordinary citizens known as plebeians—life was endured in intense poverty. Even skilled artisans and craftspeople could barely sustain their households. Women had few rights and were mostly regarded as the property of their fathers or husbands.

Even worse off were the city's throngs of beggars as well as those who were captured in battle or kidnapped from their conquered lands. They were sent back to Rome to toil as slaves. Says University of Oxford professor Barry Cunliffe, "Of all the peoples of the ancient world the Romans can the most easily be understood, for we are not looking just at dead ruins or serried ranks of dreary pottery in museum showcases but at real people—at intimate emotions, conflicts of loyalty, and incredible bravery; at ambition, naked power, and human failing."[1]

# History's First Republic

To study Rome one must study its leaders. Among Rome's most well-known emperors are those who helped build Rome into its place in history: Augustus, who expanded the empire and ended years of civil war; Vespasian, who erected many of Rome's most impressive buildings, including the Colosseum; and Titus, who reigned for just two years but is regarded as the most generous of Rome's emperors because he fed the poor and took other measures to relieve their terrible poverty. However, the list of Roman emperors also includes madmen and tyrants: Caligula and Nero—cruel and inhumane men whose reigns were marked by their personal vanities, fears of betrayal, and disregard for human rights.

Rome's ancient history spanned more than 1,200 years, from the eighth century BC to the fifth century AD. For a large portion of that time, Rome was also a republic—the first representational government in recorded history. Citizens could vote and elect members to the Senate as well as plebeian assemblies. For hundreds of years the Senate and the assemblies were the guiding forces of Roman government.

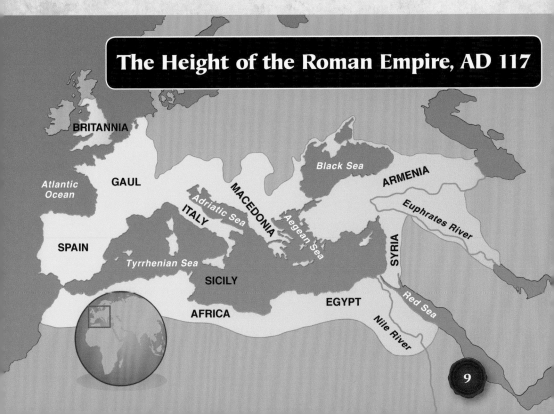

## The Height of the Roman Empire, AD 117

BRITANNIA

Atlantic Ocean

GAUL

Black Sea

ARMENIA

Adriatic Sea

MACEDONIA

ITALY

Aegean Sea

Euphrates River

SPAIN

Tyrrhenian Sea

SYRIA

SICILY

EGYPT

Red Sea

AFRICA

Nile River

Legislators created a system of laws that required obedience from everybody—rich and poor alike. Over the centuries, as Rome fell under the control of dictators and emperors, the Senate and assemblies found themselves with fewer powers, and yet centuries later, as the founding fathers of American democracy searched for inspiration, they found it in the principles of the Roman republic. Said Thomas Jefferson, "In designing the Constitution of these United States of America, we have at various times sought precedent in the history of that ancient [Roman] Republic, and endeavored to draw lessons both from its leading ideas and the tumult and factions which finally brought it low."[2]

## Religion and Warfare

One of the principles of Rome adopted into American culture was the concept of religious pluralism. For much of their ancient history, the Romans worshipped pagan gods—but they were always ready to accept other gods into Roman thought. When the Romans conquered an enemy, that enemy's peoples and treasures became Roman, but so did the enemy's gods. This dedication to religious pluralism had its limits, though. Not until the rule of Emperor Constantine in the fourth century AD would Romans accept Christianity. Until then, the Christians endured several periods of severe persecution by the Romans; most Christians were forced to practice their faith underground, often observing the rites of Christianity in the dark catacombs found beneath Roman streets.

Throughout much its history, Rome was at war—at first conquering vast swaths of territory in Europe, the Middle East, and North Africa and then defending its land against barbarians, Middle Eastern tribespeople, and other invaders who challenged Roman rule. Civil war was a frequent occurrence. Assassination was a common way to end an emperor's reign. Greed, corruption, and lust for power were rampant. Says Cunliffe, "Deep within the body of Rome lay the seeds of its own destruction. Under-production, a dependence on a slave economy, depopulation, and the upkeep of a vast standing army—all contributed to the escalating economic crisis which was gradually gaining momentum."[3]

*Slaves wearing tags indicating they are to be sold await their new masters at a slave market in ancient Rome. Rome's wealthiest citizens enjoyed art and literature and the other advantages of their social class while many of its poorest citizens toiled as slaves.*

## Gladiatorial Contests

To distract people from their poverty as well as the wars and intrigues that plagued the empire, the emperors as well as other prominent citizens often staged gladiatorial contests and other blood sports in public arenas, the largest of which was the Colosseum. These diversions helped Rome's patricians control their unruly citizens for generations, but by the fifth century AD, the Romans were incapable of managing their large and unwieldy realm.

By then Rome itself was no longer the capital of the empire. Moreover, the city had been sacked by barbarians who faced little resistance against a Roman army too weary to fight. For at least 600 years of its 1200-year history Rome had been the dominant civilization on Earth. Never again would a single society rule so much of the planet for so long a time.

# Chapter 1

# What Conditions Led to the Rise of Ancient Rome?

**W**riting in the first century BC the Roman poet Virgil crafted a story about the founding of Rome. His poem, the *Aeneid*, tells of the hero Aeneas. Escaping the sack of Troy by the Greek king Agamemnon, Aeneas leads the survivors on a sea journey that eventually ends in central Italy with the establishment of a settlement that will grow into the city of Rome. During the journey, Aeneas and his followers must endure warfare, supernatural events, and intrigues among the gods, but in the end the settlers prevail. Wrote Virgil in the opening lines of the poem:

> He suffered greatly in war until he could found
>
> A city and bring his gods to Latium, whence
>
> The Latins would spring, the Alban fathers, and Rome
>
> With its lofty walls.[4]

The *Aeneid* is regarded as an important work of classic literature: It is required reading in many high school and college humanities classes. Though it is fiction, some historians believe it actually tells a portion of the story of the beginnings of Rome.

## Romulus and Remus

According to a companion legend, Rome was founded by the twins Romulus and Remus. Said to be descendants of Aeneas, they were tossed as babies into the Tiber River, were washed ashore, and eventually found by a she-wolf who nurtured and raised them as her cubs. Romulus and Remus grew into fierce warriors and, in the year 753 BC, led their followers to a bend in the Tiber River, where they founded their city.

The two brothers quarreled about who should be king. Unable to decide on who should rule the new city, the brothers asked a group of priests, known as the augurs, to name the king. The augurs instructed the brothers to stand atop two of the city's hills. When a group of birds flocked over Romulus, the augurs declared him king.

Unable to accept the decision, Remus challenged Romulus. The two brothers fought. Romulus won the battle, slaying his brother. He named the new city Roma, after himself, and started building his settlement atop the Palatine, one of the seven hills of Rome. Says Barry Cunliffe, "Thus in violence and fratricide, according to the legends, the city of Rome was born."[5]

## Land of the Golden Sunlight

Historians say the truth about the founding of Rome can probably be found in both the *Aeneid* and the legend of the twins. Like Aeneas, it is likely that sailors traveled west from Athens in Greece or Tyre in Lebanon, arriving at the Italian Peninsula. The Greek sailors called the land Hesperia, after the goddesses known as the Hesperides who ruled over the golden sunlight. And although the supernatural portions of the story of Romulus and Remus may be subject to skepticism, it is likely that a strong leader—if not Romulus himself then somebody with the warrior skills of Romulus—is likely to have led his followers to a settlement along the Tiber River in the eighth century BC.

For the earliest settlers, it was a tough and hardscrabble way of life. In later years the Romans built such magnificent examples of architecture as the Colosseum and the Forum, but at this stage they were likely to have been living in mud huts. They were a brutish and uncivilized people at home living in the wild. As such, women were loathe to live among the Romans.

*In the centuries-old poem, the* Aeneid, *the hero Aeneas (pictured with his soldiers in this twentieth-century engraving), escapes the sack of Troy and leads survivors to central Italy. There they establish a settlement that will one day be known as Rome.*

According to legend, Romulus hatched a scheme to supply child-bearing wives to his male followers—he planned the abduction of women from nearby villages. He staged a festival and invited neighboring tribes to attend. Among those who attended the festival were members of a tribe known as the Sabines.

# Rape of the Sabine Women

Roman legend holds that during the festival's games, Romulus's men abducted and raped the Sabine women and drove off the men. The Sabine men soon returned in force and attacked Rome. They were able to enter Rome with the help of the Sabine woman Tarpeia, who threw open the gates of the city. According to the legend, Tarpeia was crushed by the Sabine men as they rushed to enter. (In later generations her name would be associated with the Tarpeian Rock, the stony ridge in Rome where condemned men were hurled to their deaths.)

As the two armies clashed, the Sabine women, fearing their husbands and fathers would die at the hands of the Romans, pleaded for peace. Romulus and the Sabine king, Tatius, met in a part of the city that would later serve as the Roman Forum. They agreed to an armistice, with the Sabines becoming Romans and the two kings ruling together until Tatius's death five years later. Says author and Pennsylvania State University English professor Steven Bonta, "Romulus is depicted as a warlike individual, the most ruthless member of a very rough crowd. The stories of his murder of Remus, his brother, and his war with the Sabines over the rape of the Sabine women by his men, whether true or not, are certainly in keeping with the warlike spirit the Romans cultivated, from the very foundation of their city."[6]

Romulus is said to have died in 717 BC—he was 52 years old and had ruled for 36 years. According to legend, the war god Mars swept down to earth and carried the king off to heaven in a whirlwind. A scholar of the era named Julius Proculus claimed to have been visited by the spirit of Romulus as the king ascended to heaven. According to Proculus, the spirit of Romulus told him, "Go and tell the Romans that by heaven's will my Rome shall be capital of the world. Let them learn to be soldiers. Let them know, and teach their children, that no power on earth can stand against Roman arms."[7]

# The City Expands

To assist in his rule, Romulus established a 100-member advisory council, composed of the leaders of Rome's most prominent families. This council was known as the Senate. Following the death of Romulus, the Senate remained intact, assisting other kings and wielding considerable influence in the affairs of the city.

Among the successors to Romulus were the kings Numa Pompilius, who presided over an era of peace; Tullus Hostilius, under whom Rome expanded, doubling in size as he attacked and conquered nearby cities and made their citizens into Romans, and Ancus Marcius, who further expanded the boundaries of the city by waging war on Rome's neighbors. Writing in AD 29, the Roman historian Titus Livius, known familiarly as Livy, said, "Numa had established religious observances in time of peace; Ancus provided war with an equivalent solemn ceremonial of its own."[8]

These kings helped make Rome larger and more powerful, but far from the masters of the Italian Peninsula that the Romans would eventually become. Even before the founding of Rome, Italy was ruled by a civilization known as the Etruscans, whose kingdom was based in the region north of Rome that is today known as Tuscany. It is likely that from the Etruscans, the Romans developed their taste for blood sports—the Etruscans often staged sporting events during the funerals of important people. The first gladiators were probably Etruscan wrestlers—slaves captured during warfare. The Etruscans also developed mines, finding valuable ores such as iron, copper, and tin. And they were a seafaring people who sailed as far away as Syria and Portugal to conduct trade.

## Rule of the Etruscans

Since the earliest days of Rome, the Etruscans had granted the city a measure of independence and self-rule, but eventually Etruscan rulers moved to Rome and established their dominance over the city. The first Etruscan to rule Rome was Lucius Tarquinius Priscus, who, legend holds, entered the city as a humble plebeian riding in an oxcart. He rose in prominence and wealth and, upon the death of Ancus in 616 BC, seized power with the help of wealthy and powerful Etruscan families. Wrote Livy, "In most ways he was a man of

# Titus Livius, Historian of Ancient Rome

**M**uch of the history of ancient Rome was recorded by Titus Livius, known more familiarly as Livy. He lived from 59 BC to AD 17 and wrote during the reign of Emperor Augustus.

Augustus came to power during an era of civil war and dissent in Rome. It was his intention to bring peace to the empire, and he called on Livy to write a history of early Rome trumpeting the great triumphs of the Romans as a way of lifting the morale of the Roman people. Livy was happy to oblige his emperor.

During his lifetime Livy produced the massive *History of Rome from Its Foundation*, which was first published in 29 BC. It is believed Livy produced 142 volumes, although just 35 have survived.

Historians who have studied Livy's works have found many inaccuracies and contradictory facts. In one case he underestimated the number of soldiers killed in a Greek campaign by 30,000; in another case, he confused the names of the Greek cities Thermon and Thermopylae.

Nevertheless, historians believe his engaging prose has given life to Roman history. Says author and Pennsylvania State University English professor Steven Bonta, "As with most ancient authors, much of Livy's Roman history has been lost, but the remaining portions are packed with fascinating details and vivid descriptions of pivotal events."

Steven Bonta, "The Birth of the Republic," *New American*, October 4, 2004.

outstanding character and ability; nevertheless . . . he was something of a schemer."[9]

It was under Priscus that some of Rome's most familiar and grandest buildings and monuments rose. Priscus erected the Temple of Jupiter on the Capitoline Hill as well as a venue for games and chariot races known as the Circus Maximus. Construction of the Roman Forum, which would serve as the seat of Roman government for the next several centuries, began under the reign of Priscus.

But Priscus lost the throne, falling victim to what would become a common method for ousting Roman rulers: assassination. Indeed, he would be killed on the orders of aristocrats who feared he was becoming too powerful. Priscus was succeeded by his son, Servius Tullius, who shared his father's desire to build impressive structures, the grandest of which was the Servian Wall, a 5-mile-long (8km) wall that encircled the city, providing a measure of security against Rome's enemies.

In 560 BC Servius authorized the first census of Roman citizens. The census established each Roman's status as a citizen of the city and also detailed his or her obligations with regard to taxes, laws, and military service. In a civilization otherwise ruled by kings and aristocrats, these were important rights that gave each citizen of Rome a measure of equality. The census and the influence of the Senate did not bring wide-ranging democracy to Rome—the Etruscan kings and aristocrats still held tremendous power over the Romans—but these reforms would lay the groundwork for the future creation of the Roman republic.

## Tarquin the Proud

In 534 BC Servius's brother-in-law, Tarquinius Superbus, or Tarquin the Proud, challenged the king's authority. Hoping to silence Tarquinius, Servius staged an election, asking the people of Rome whether he should remain as king. Servius declared the results showed him with nothing less than unanimous support. Tarquinius was unimpressed with what was obviously a rigged election and ordered Servius assassinated, taking the throne for himself.

Tarquinius was far less interested in reform and democracy than Servius. Tarquinius was a despotic and domineering tyrant. "Under Tarquinius Superbus the monarchy became absolute, and Etruscan influence supreme," says historian Will Durant. "He surrounded himself with a bodyguard, degraded freemen with months of forced labor, had citizens crucified in the Forum, put to death many leaders of the upper classes, and ruled with an insolent brutality that won him the hatred of all influential men."[10]

Despite ruling with a cruel hand, Tarquin, like his predecessors, oversaw construction of many Roman monuments and buildings while also extending Rome's influence over other Italian cities. Wrote Livy, "However lawless and tyrannical Tarquin may have been as monarch in his own country, as a war leader he did fine work. Indeed, his fame as a soldier might have equaled that of his predecessors, had not his degeneracy in other things obscured its luster."[11]

Tarquin ruled Rome for a quarter of a century. He was the last of the so-called Seven Kings of Rome, the initial line of Roman rulers that commenced with Romulus nearly 250 years earlier.

## Rebellion in Rome

The spark that ignited the rebellion against Etruscan rule was lit when Lucretia, the wife of a Roman noble, was raped by Tarquinius's son Sextus. After the assault, Lucretia summoned her husband, Lucius Tarquinius Collatinus, as well as her father and her husband's close friend, Lucius Junius Brutus. She tearfully informed her husband and the others of the rape, then drew a knife and committed suicide. More than 2,000 years later, William Shakespeare told the story of the assault in his lengthy poem *The Rape of Lucrece*. In the poem, Brutus calls on Romans to avenge the death of Lucretia and oust the Etruscan dynasty:

Kneel with me and help to bear thy part

To rouse our Roman gods with invocations

That they will suffer these abominations,

Since Rome herself in them doth stand disgraced.[12]

Riots soon broke out in the city while Brutus organized a revolt among Roman soldiers in the Etruscan army. The Roman soldiers turned on Tarquinius and drove him out of Rome. The despot fled to the Etruscan city of Veii about 10 miles (16km) north of Rome. He raised an army and marched on Rome but was repelled.

The struggle for control of Rome would continue for another four years. Tarquin had now taken refuge in the city of Gabii, about 10 miles (16km) east of Rome. He sent spies into the city, hoping to spark revolution and clear the way for him to return to power. Among the conspirators recruited by Tarquin's spies were two teenage sons of Brutus. The plot was uncovered and Brutus was forced to preside over the execution of his sons—the boys were flogged and beheaded.

## Rome's First Hero

In 506 BC an Etruscan prince named Lars Porsena marched on Rome, capturing territory west of the Tiber River. All that separated Porsena from the city was a bridge spanning the Tiber that was defended by a small force of soldiers under the leadership of an officer named Horatius Cocles.

To defend Rome against the advancing Etruscans, Cocles strode halfway across the bridge and ordered his men to destroy the bridge behind him. Wrote Livy, "Looking round with eyes dark with menace upon the Etruscan chiefs, he challenged them to single combat, and reproached them all with being the slaves of tyrant kings."[13] According to legend, Cocles held off the charging Etruscans singlehandedly until, finally, the bridge collapsed beneath him. Miraculously, Cocles survived the fall and was able to swim back to the Roman side of the river as Etruscan arrows darted around him.

Many historians question the truthfulness in the story of Cocles's defense of Rome, believing it contains a large dose of myth. Nevertheless, for his efforts in saving the city, Cocles was awarded a large tract of land, the erection of a statue in his honor, and a place in history as Rome's first military hero.

## Birth of the Republic

During the initial chaos after the ouster of Tarquinius, the Senate convened and declared that Romans would never again live under the authority of a king: Romans would govern themselves. Moreover, every Roman citizen would have a vote. The city would be a *res publica*—in English, a "public affair," or "republic." While it was not the first democracy in history—in the Greek city-state of Athens, citizens cast votes directly for laws—the Roman republic was the first representative democracy. The government would be run by elected leaders, members of the Senate, who in turn selected two superior leaders to serve as consuls.

The consuls were the actual heads of the Roman government—the position is similar to a president or prime minister. The first two

*Horses pound the turf as charioteers compete for victory in a Roman chariot race. Chariot races and other competitive events took place in the Circus Maximus, one of the many grand structures built during the reign of the Etruscan ruler Priscus.*

consuls were Brutus and Lucretia's husband, Collatinus. The Senate elected to place authority in the hands of two leaders as a check on power—the senators did not want to give absolute authority to one person.

Collatinus served as consul only briefly. He was related to Tarquinius and feared that by remaining in authority, Romans would suspect that he owed allegiance to the Etruscan king. Collatinus was soon replaced by Publius Valerius, who drafted some of the first laws establishing equal rights for Roman citizens. (He became known as Publicola, or "friend of the people.") Among the laws written by Valerius were the establishment of the death penalty for anybody who attempted to make himself king as well as anybody who tried to take public office without consent of the people. Valerius also drafted a law granting rights of appeal to condemned prisoners, and he lowered taxes for poor citizens.

## The People's Assembly

Despite the efforts of such reformers as Valerius, following the overthrow of Tarquinius it seemed to most plebeians that they were no better off under the aristocrats of Rome than they had been under the Etruscan kings. In 494 BC the people of Rome staged what became known as the First Plebeian Secession. Essentially, it was a citywide strike of all working people. (Over the next 200 years, the Roman plebeians would stage four more strikes.) Shops shut down while craftspeople and laborers stopped working. Many plebeians left the city and made their way to a nearby mountain, taking something of a holiday while leaving the aristocrats to fend for themselves in the city.

The Roman Senate responded to their concerns, establishing the office of tribune to represent the interests of the working people in the government of Rome. The tribunes—eventually, there were a total of 10—gave the plebeians a voice in the Roman Senate because they held veto powers over laws.

The tribunes were elected by four assemblies that met outdoors at a *comitium,* or "place of assembly." Membership in the assemblies was

Visitors to twenty-first-century Rome are hard-pressed to find the original seven hills of the city; just the hill known as the Capitoline remains discernible. However, archaeological evidence suggests that there were early settlements on all seven hills, and that each hill was surrounded by walls. The other original hills of Rome were known as the Aventine, Caelian, Esquiline, Palatine, Quirinal, and Viminal.

The oldest settlement may have been located on the Esquiline; archaeological evidence suggests it may have been inhabited by a walled city in the eighth century BC. According to legend, Remus made his home on the Aventine, while the Palatine was the hill where Romulus built the city. Later, the richest and most powerful Romans made their homes on the Palatine. The Sabines, whose women were abducted by the Romans under Romulus, established their city on the Quirinal.

The Capitoline is where the Etruscan king Lucius Tarquinius Priscus began construction of the Temple of Jupiter as a monument to the most powerful of the Roman gods. While digging the foundation, the workers unearthed the head of a man with the face intact. They regarded this as a symbol—that the temple should be the head of the empire. Wrote the Roman historian Titus Livius, "The sight of this phenomenon by no doubtful indications portended that this temple should be the seat of the empire, and the capital of the world."

John Henry Freese, Alfred John Church, and William Jackson Brodribb, trans., *Roman History by Livy.* New York: D. Appleton, 1904, p. 64.

based on a variety of factors, such as neighborhoods of residency, tribal affiliations, age, and value of property. The most influential of the assemblies was the *concilium plebis*, or People's Assembly, which met in the Forum. The *concilium plebis* could formulate resolutions, known as plebiscites; by 287 BC the People's Assembly had grown to be widely influential, and its resolutions were binding on all citizens.

## The Twelve Tables

Even with this new measure of representation, the plebeians were still not satisfied with their low status in Roman society. The Roman Senate was still composed of the wealthy and aristocratic citizens of Rome, and they interpreted the Roman laws as they desired—and usually in their favor. Plebeian leaders called on the Senate to adopt a written code of laws—a constitution—and around 450 BC the Senate complied with their demands.

The Roman constitution was not the first written code of laws in history. The Greeks, under the Athenian statesman Solon, had established such a code. Before adopting its own code of laws, the Romans dispatched a council of 10 scholars, known as the decemviri, to Athens to study the Greek laws. Returning from Athens, the decemviri drafted a code known as the Twelve Tables—a set of laws so fundamental that they would be inscribed in stone, never to be changed.

Rights guaranteed by the Twelve Tables included outlawing the death penalty without a conviction in a court as well as relief for debtors, giving them a month-long grace period before they had to repay their debts. The Twelve Tables also established rules for inheriting family wealth and established execution as the penalty for treason. Some of the laws established by the Twelve Tables may have been unduly harsh—those who committed crimes of slander or of giving false testimony in court could be put to death. The Twelve Tables also authorized the killing of deformed infants. Nevertheless, the plebeians now had their written laws. They were etched in stone and kept in the Roman Forum. Says Bonta, "The Twelve Tables became, like the English Magna Carta, a palpable symbol of Roman liberty, and they served as an effective restraint on the arbitrary interpretation of Roman law."[14]

With an elected Senate, the establishment of the People's Assembly, and a written code of laws, Rome was now truly a republic. The motto for the city became SPQR—initials for the Latin phrase *Senatus Populus Que Romanus*, which means the "Senate and Roman People." Rome had spawned the first representative government in history, establishing a course that would be followed centuries later by today's modern democracies. Unlike many of today's democracies, though, the Roman republic was built on a less solid foundation, and in time it would crumble under the whims of dictators and tyrants.

# Chapter 2

# Wars of Expansion

In the year AD 101, Emperor Trajan led an army east to the kingdom of Dacia, which could be found north of the Danube River. As the Dacian king, Decebalus, was soon to learn, the Romans were aggressive and relentless warriors who rarely backed down from an opponent. The two armies clashed first near the city of Tapae. Trajan wiped out the Dacian army, but months later Decebalus regrouped and counterattacked. Again, the Romans prevailed, and once more Decebalus was forced to retreat.

He was pursued by Trajan back to his capital of Sarmizegethusa. Surrounded by the Roman army, Decebalus sued for peace. The surrender terms were harsh: Decebalus was forced to turn over large tracts of territory to the Romans, ceding much of his kingdom to Trajan. Over the next four years, sporadic fighting would break out from time to time, but by AD 105 Decebalus had been killed in battle, the resistance was wiped out, and the people of this region were now Romans. Says Will Durant, "To reimburse himself for his labors Trajan took out of Dacia a million pounds of silver and half a million pounds of gold—the last substantial booty that the [Roman] legions would win for [Rome]."[15]

For defeating the Dacians, the Roman Senate conferred on Trajan the honorary title "Dacicus," or "conqueror of Dacia." The Senate also erected a monument to the emperor, known as Trajan's Column, that has survived the centuries and remains standing today.

As for Dacia, it acquired a new name: In the local languages it became known as Romania, which means "Land of the Romans." The country of Romania is still known by that name today.

# Spoils of War

Trajan's conquest of Dacia in AD 101 marks the last great expansion of Rome. Since winning their independence from the Etruscan kings in 509 BC, some 6 centuries before, the Romans were constantly waging war against their neighbors as well as citizens in far-off lands. During this era of expansion that ended with the invasion of Dacia, the city on the Tiber had grown into an empire that spanned across much of Europe, North Africa, and the Middle East. More than 2 million square miles (5.2 million square km) were under Roman rule. When Rome conquered a kingdom, its people became Romans. By the time Trajan defeated the Dacians, more than 4 million people lived under Roman rule.

This long era of war began when Brutus convinced the Roman soldiers to rebel against Tarquinius. This was not a brief campaign by the Romans: They would wage war against the Etruscans for a century, finally wiping out all remnants of Etruscan rule while taking over much of the Italian Peninsula. In 396 BC Rome defeated the city of Veii, overrunning the last of the Etruscan strongholds.

During this era of warfare, noncombatants suffered as much as soldiers. When the Romans took a city, citizens were often put to death, taken as slaves, or driven from their homes while the city was sacked— its wealth pillaged by the invaders.

# Kindness of a General

An exception to this style of combat occurred soon after the fall of Veii when the Roman general Marcus Furius Camillus attacked the city of Falerii about 30 miles (48km) north of Rome. The city was walled and well fortified, and Camillus's army was unable to breach the gates. However, a traitorous schoolmaster inside the city tricked a group of schoolchildren into following him through the gates; he then turned the children over to the Romans and suggested the students could be used as hostages to force the city to surrender.

When Camillus learned of the schoolmaster's act of treachery, he ordered the traitor brought before him. Livy writes that Camillus was appalled by the schoolmaster's plan to harm innocent children. "War also has laws even as peace, and to these laws we have learnt obedience, even as we have learned courage," Camillus told the schoolmaster. "Our arms we carry not against lads of tender age, who are not harmed even in storming of cities, but against men that carry arms in their hands."[16] Camillus ordered the man stripped and bound. He then gave the schoolchildren whips and prods, allowing them to beat their teacher and drive him back into the city.

The citizens of Falerii, awed by the kindness displayed by Camillus, surrendered to this noblest of Roman generals. In return, Camillus ordered his men not to sack the city. While this story would seem to have a fairy tale ending, that is not the case. Camillus's men, angered that they were denied the spoils of war, grew to hate their commander. And when Camillus returned to Rome, he found the city's political leaders angry with him as well. In prior battles, whenever a Roman army conquered a city, Roman citizens were permitted to move into the vanquished city and take over the vacant homes left behind by those who were either murdered, enslaved, or driven out by the Roman soldiers. But Camillus's act of kindness to the people of Falerii had denied Roman citizens their spoils. Back in Rome, Camillus found himself hounded and shunned; he eventually resigned from the army and went into exile.

## Defeated by the Gauls

The Romans were not alone in waging war against their enemies—and showing little mercy to their vanquished foes. A little more than a century after winning independence from the Etruscans, Rome suffered one of its rare military defeats when tribes of Gauls rode south into Italy, attacking and overrunning cities. Enemy soldiers as well as women and children were ruthlessly murdered by the Gallic tribespeople, who were based in a region of what is now France.

In 387 BC the Gauls laid siege to the city of Clusium, about 100 miles (161km) north of Rome. Clusium was an Etruscan city. Its leaders, believing they had more to fear from the Gauls than from their

# Siege at Masada

Among the Middle Eastern states conquered by Rome was the nation of Judea, located roughly where the modern state of Israel can be found. The Romans found it a difficult nation to govern mostly because its Jewish citizens refused to accept Rome's pagan religion. Also, the Romans instituted harsh taxes on Judea and helped themselves to the national treasury. In AD 66, Judea erupted in rebellion.

Thousands of Jews and many Roman soldiers died in the rebellion. Still, within two years the Jews gained control of Judea's largest city, Jerusalem. In response, the Roman emperor Vespasian dispatched an army to retake Jerusalem and put down the uprising. The army was led by Vespasian's son Titus, a future emperor.

The army laid siege to the city; for five months, the Roman soldiers hunted down the rebels. More than 100,000 were killed, and another 97,000 were caught and sent back to Rome as slaves.

In AD 73 the final 960 holdouts took refuge in a fortress atop a rocky plateau in southern Judea. They remained in the fortress, known as Masada, for several months. To gain access to the fortress, the Romans built a tower atop a pile of dirt and rock so they could lay a ramp over the wall. After gaining access to the fortress, though, the Romans discovered that nearly all the rebels were dead. The Jews had taken their own lives rather than face slavery in Rome.

old enemies the Romans, sent a message to Rome asking for help. The Romans responded by dispatching three emissaries to Clusium to negotiate a treaty with the Gallic leader Brennus.

Brennus suspected the three emissaries were spies, sent by Rome to assess the strength of his army. Whatever the intentions of the Romans, the meeting did not go well. The Romans and Gauls exchanged insults, swords were drawn, and a Gallic tribal leader was killed. The Roman emissaries fled, followed close behind by a horde of angry Gauls.

Eleven miles (17.7km) north of Rome, the Gauls encountered the Roman army, which had been dispatched to defend the city. The Romans were outnumbered and outfought, and the Gauls easily overran the defenders. Many of the Roman soldiers managed to escape the massacre and flee back to Rome, where they took refuge on the Capitoline, which was well fortified. Below the Capitoline fortifications, the Gauls poured into the city, looting and burning everything in sight. They remained in Rome for seven months, attempting many times to dislodge the remaining soldiers from the Capitoline but failing each time.

Finally, the Romans sued for peace. The price demanded by Brennus was high—1,000 pounds (454kg) of gold—but the Romans felt they had no choice and agreed to the Gallic leader's demands. To add humiliation to the defeat, the Gauls weighed the gold with scales that were tipped in their favor. When the Roman general Quintus Sulpicius protested, Brennus barked *"Vae victis!"*[17] ("Woe to the vanquished!") and threw his sword onto the scale, further tipping the weight to the Gauls' advantage.

## The Roman Legions

It was a humiliating defeat—one of only a handful of defeats that would be suffered by the Romans over the next 800 years. The Romans learned from their experience at the hands of the Gauls. They rebuilt their city and also rebuilt their army.

At first, the army was composed of conscripts—all able-bodied men were expected to serve in the army as a duty of citizenship. Eventually, Roman military leaders ensured that army veterans would receive tracts of land in payment for their services. This was known as the *honoraria* and was paid upon a soldier's honorable discharge. As the empire spread to regions far distant from Rome, the army was converted to an all-volunteer professional fighting force. The army became a lifelong career. For many Roman men, military service was their only path out of poverty.

The Roman generals learned from their enemies, copying their tactics and their weaponry. From the Greeks, the Romans adopted the use of spears and round shields. From the Gauls, the Romans learned to use a javelin known as a *pilum* along with a larger, oblong shield and chain-mail armor. From the Etruscans, the Romans copied the makeup of the armies, dividing their military into units composed of about 5,000 soldiers. These units were known as the Roman legions.

The Roman general and consul Gaius Marius, who lived from 157 to 86 BC, is regarded as most responsible for making the Roman army into the world's most feared fighting force. "He was a soldier, not a statesman," says Durant. "He had no time to weigh distant political consequences. He led his recruits . . . hardened their bodies with marches and drills, and developed their courage with attacks upon objectives that could easily be won."[18]

Marius and the other Roman generals knew the value of well-fed, rested, and healthy soldiers—an army in the best physical condition held an edge over the enemy. The army was also disciplined. If a soldier deserted or showed cowardice in battle, the whole legion suffered. To answer for cowardice, hundreds of otherwise brave men were selected for punishment that could include beatings, floggings, or death by stoning.

## Tactics of the Roman Army

Although trained to be fierce warriors, face-to-face combat was, for the Romans, the tactic of last resort. To lay siege to an enemy city, which was usually walled, the Roman army preferred instead to encircle the city and starve the inhabitants into submission. Said the fourth-century-AD Roman military tactician Flavius Vegetius Renatus, "To distress the enemy more by famine than by sword is the mark of consummate skill."[19]

Starving the enemy into surrendering could often take several months. To help speed things up, the Romans would use catapults to fling the rotting carcasses of livestock over the city walls, spreading plague and other diseases. Rocks, spears, and other projectiles would also be hurled over the walls.

When combat occurred on an open field, Roman generals employed tactics they devised and recorded in military manuals. Among Roman generals, the most valued of these manuals was *The Stratagemata*, written by Sextus Julius Frontinus (who also designed Rome's water supply system). *The Stratagemata* and other manuals covered such issues as attacking with the sun to the Roman army's back in order to blind the enemy, using the advantage of the wind to help propel arrows, and the importance of always holding men in reserve to join the battle later, if needed.

One familiar tactic was the use of the wedge, which required the army to enter the battle in a formation that resembled a triangle. The point of the wedge would thrust into the enemy lines first, followed by more and more soldiers as the wedge expanded. This formation would usually divide the enemy's forces, making them weaker.

Indeed, the combat tactics of the day required men to fight toe to toe, sword to sword. Since it was much easier to kill a man from behind, the Roman soldiers were drilled never to turn their backs, thus exposing their most vulnerable sides to the enemy. This rule meant that Roman soldiers never ran away from a fight—they were expected to kill the enemy soldier after he gave up and retreated, usually with a sword or javelin thrust to the back.

## The First Punic War

These tactics served the Roman army well. During the height of the empire's influence, the Roman army numbered some 500,000 soldiers. Following the defeat by the Gauls, the Roman legions would suffer occasional defeats, to be sure, but those were typically avenged as military commanders regrouped, summoned reserves, and attacked again with a relentless resolve to vanquish their foes. No enemy of Rome would learn the extent of Roman military might more than the city-state in North Africa known as Carthage.

Located in what is today Tunisia, Carthage was originally a colony of the Phoenicians—inhabitants of modern-day Lebanon, Syria, and Israel. Around 575 BC, as Phoenician society fell into decline, the Carthaginians won their independence and soon grew to dominate North Africa. The Carthaginians were a seafaring people—they built a massive navy that ferried goods for trade across the Mediterranean. However, the Romans considered them a race of thugs—the Carthaginian religion required the sacrifice of children. Still, there was no denying the wealth and influence of Carthage. Describing the city of Carthage, Durant says:

> The city, crowded with a quarter of a million inhabitants, became famous for its gleaming temples, its public baths, above all for its secure harbors and spacious docks. . . . Houses rose to six stories, and often crowded a family into a single room. In the center of the city, providing one of many hints to the later builders of Rome, stood a hill or citadel—the Bysra; here were

## The First and Second Punic Wars

Lake Trasimeno (217)
Trabbia (218)
Po River
Metaurus (207)
Sena Gallica
Alps
Liguria
Adriatic Sea
Bay of Biscay
Pyrenees
Etruria
Nola (215)
Cannae (216)
Ebro River
Corsica
Rome
CAMPANIA
Apulia
SPAIN
Capus
Tarentum
Tagus River
Saguntum (219)
Balearic Islands
Sardinia
Panormus (254)
Mylae
Drepanum (249)
(260)
Croton
Baecula (208)
Cape Hermaeum (255)
Locri
Llipa (206)
Carthago Nova (209)
Mediterranean Sea
Utica (204)
Carthage
Sicily
Messana (263)
Syracuse
Tunis (255)
Cape Ecnomus (256)
Clypea
Agrigentum (282)
NUMIDIA
Zama (202)
Lilybaeum (241)

| | | |
|---|---|---|
| Carthaginian territory about 270 BC | → | Hannibal's route about 270 BC |
| Roman territory about 270 BC | ■ | Battlesite with year of battle (BC) |

0 ——— 200 mi
0 ——— 300 km

the Treasury and the Mint, more shrines and colonnades, and the most brilliant of Carthaginian temples—to the great god Eshmun. Around the landward side of the city ran a threefold protective wall forty-five feet high, with still higher towers and battlements; within the wall were accommodations for 4,000 horses, 300 elephants, and 20,000 men. Outside the walls were the estates of the rich, and beyond these, the fields of the poor.[20]

In 264 BC a regional dispute between pirates who used the island of Sicily as a base and the Greek colony of Syracuse, also located on Sicily, erupted into the First Punic War. (*Punic* was the Romans' term for the Carthaginians—their eventual enemies in the conflict. It was also the language spoken by the Carthaginians.) The Romans saw this conflict as a way to gain control of Sicily and at first sided with the Greeks, but their real plan was to rid the western half of Sicily of the Carthaginians. The pirates turned to the Carthaginians for help against the Greeks and Romans but eventually betrayed Carthage and gave their allegiance to Rome.

## The Second Punic War

Rome attempted to attack Carthage, but the Roman legions were turned away. Retreating back across the Mediterranean, the Roman army instead concentrated on ousting the Carthaginians from Sicily. At the time the war broke out, Rome did not have a navy, but after capturing a Carthaginian ship, the Romans copied it and were able to construct a navy of several hundred ships, which they used effectively against the Carthaginians.

The war dragged on until 241 BC, when Carthage finally relented and agreed to give up all claims to Sicily. The Carthaginians also agreed to pay a massive penalty to Rome and cease trading in waters controlled by the Roman navy.

When the First Punic War ended, a Carthaginian child named Hannibal was 7 years old. He was just 30 years old in the year 218 BC, but by then he was already the military leader of Carthage. That

# A Pyrrhic Victory

The term "Pyrrhic victory" is used to describe a victory won at a high cost. The term stems from a battle waged against the Romans by Pyrrhus, king of Epirus, which is a region that now makes up portions of Greece and Albania.

In 280 BC Pyrrhus responded to a call for aid from the Greek inhabitants of the city of Tarentum in southern Italy, which was under threat by a Roman army. Pyrrhus attacked the Romans near the city of Heraclea. Pyrrhus led an army of some 30,000, whereas the Roman army numbered 35,000. Despite the slight edge in manpower, the Romans soon fell back in retreat, mostly because Pyrrhus sent waves of elephants against the Roman cavalry. The Romans lost as many as 15,000 soldiers, and Pyrrhus lost 11,000 men. Following the battle, Pyrrhus is said to have remarked, "One more such victory and we are lost."

Pyrrhus replenished his ranks and advanced north. Within a few months he again encountered a Roman army. He won the battle but once again suffered many casualties—another 11,000 of his soldiers were killed.

Pyrrhus would face a Roman army one final time—at the Italian city of Beneventum in 275 BC. This time, he lost. By now the Romans were the unquestioned rulers of southern Italy. Following the battle, Pyrrhus returned to his kingdom. He was killed in a street brawl in 272 BC.

Quoted in Terrence Poulos, *Extreme War: The Biggest, Best, Bloodiest, and Worst in Warfare.* New York: Kensington, 2004, p. 77.

year, Hannibal led a force of 40,000 soldiers across the Mediterranean to attack Rome and avenge the defeat of Carthage in the First Punic War.

At first, it seemed as though the Second Punic War would be won swiftly by the Carthaginians. Hannibal led his army, which included a herd of elephants, through Spain and across the Alps, then south into Italy. Over a two-year span, Hannibal's army clashed four times with Roman soldiers, winning decisive victories in each encounter. Hannibal's soldiers then settled in for a long occupation of the Italian Peninsula, edging closer to the walls of Rome. "It must have seemed that Rome was finished," says Barry Cunliffe. "But for some reason, perhaps because of lack of support from the Italian towns, Hannibal's overwhelming victories were not followed up; it is almost as though in the moment of his success his resolve had begun to falter. . . . The time was now ripe for a major Roman initiative—the war was to be taken to Carthage."[21]

## The Fall of Carthage

In 204 BC the Roman general Publius Scipio Africanus led an army across the Mediterranean to stage a counterattack against Carthage. Hannibal was forced to withdraw his army from Italy and return to Africa to defend the homeland. The decisive battle was staged near the city of Zama. The Romans, aided by local tribesmen known as the Numidians, defeated Hannibal's army. The surrender terms were harsh: Carthage was forced to cede most of its North African territory to Rome as well as vast quantities of gold and other treasures. The Carthaginian fleet was destroyed while Hannibal fled in exile to Greece, where he remained in hiding until his death by suicide in 183 BC.

Carthage suffered its final defeat at Roman hands half a century later. Since the end of the Second Punic War, Carthage had tried to rebuild itself, but the city constantly suffered attacks by Numidians, who were supported by Rome. In 149 BC Rome sent an army to North Africa to support the Numidians, and three years later the Roman army wiped out the Carthaginians, ending the very brief Third Punic War.

"For at least 10 days the city burned," Cunliffe says of the end of Carthage. "Finally what little remained standing was leveled and the last symbolic act took place: the site was cursed and a plough drawn across the rubble scratching a furrow into which salt was thrown, to signify that Carthage should forever remain barren."[22]

*The Carthaginian leader Hannibal, atop an elephant, leads his army into Italy. Hannibal's troops won several decisive victories against the Romans but ultimately suffered defeat.*

# Caesar the Conqueror

Decades after the fall of Carthage, the Romans aimed to avenge their defeat by the Gauls. Indeed, for some 300 years the humiliating Gallic victory over Rome had festered in the minds of many Roman leaders. Starting in 58 BC, a young military leader named Gaius Julius Caesar led an army into Europe. He conquered vast territories that now include France and Great Britain and was particularly harsh on the Gauls, killing 1 million and enslaving another million.

The decisive battle occurred in 52 BC at the city of Alesia, which was located near what is today the city of Dijon in eastern France. A Gallic leader, Vercingetorix, led a revolt that massacred several Roman officials. Caesar retaliated, but his initial attack was turned back by the Gauls, who were able to cut off the Romans from fresh supplies of food and men. At first, things looked bleak for the Roman army.

Caesar had been caught off guard, but the Roman general would prove his genius as a tactician. When Vercingetorix established his base at the top of a hill, Caesar ordered the hill surrounded. He directed his soldiers to encircle the hill with ditches—some 9 miles (14.5km) were dug, bottling up a force of 80,000 Gauls. Now Caesar could fall back on the old Roman tactic of starving an enemy into submission.

As Vercingetorix's men grew weak with hunger, a reserve of 250,000 Gallic fighters approached Alesia. Caesar was outnumbered, but his men fought bravely and the battle soon turned in the Romans' favor. Indeed, the Roman soldiers fought relentlessly and without mercy, slaughtering the attacking Gauls. Witnessing the carnage from the top of the hill, Vercingetorix realized all was lost. A day after the battle of Alesia, Vercingetorix surrendered. He was taken back to Rome in chains and imprisoned for the next six years and later murdered.

Five years after defeating the Gauls at Alesia, Caesar extended his campaign into Pontus (a part of modern Turkey) where he is said to have uttered these words after winning an important battle:

"*Veni, vidi, vici.*"[23] In English his words translate to, "I came, I saw, I conquered."

Rome's many wars had widened the boundaries of the powerful city-state beyond the Italian Peninsula. At the height of its power, Rome controlled vast territories across three continents—Europe, Asia, and Africa. But there is no question that Rome had also over-extended itself—eventually, the Roman legions would not be used to conquer new territories but to put down rebellions and control the many unruly peoples who bristled under the authority of their Roman masters.

# Chapter 3

# The Roman Empire at Its Height

To satisfy his citizens' thirst for blood sports and entertainment, in the year AD 72 Emperor Vespasian ordered construction of one of ancient Rome's most magnificent structures: the Colosseum. The emperor did not live to see its completion—the Colosseum took eight years to build and was finished under the authority of Vespasian's son and successor, Titus.

The impressive structure reflects the architectural skills of the ancient Romans. The circular amphitheater stands four stories high and could accommodate more than 50,000 spectators.

"The 'best people' naturally occupied the best seats, and in the Empire the Emperor with his attendants occupied the best seats of all," says John Percy Balsdon, professor of ancient history at Exeter College in England. "He was conspicuous especially in the amphitheater, since it was he who was the patron who [sponsored the games]."[24] Sitting near the emperor were the members of the Senate and other high-ranking patricians (aristocrats). Seated just above the senators were the equestrians, another class of aristocrats who ranked just below the patricians.

Occupying the tiers of seats above the equestrians were the unruly throngs of plebeian (commoners) spectators. Gambling was common in these seats as Romans wagered on the outcomes of the games unfolding before them. The top tiers of seats were occupied by slaves, foreigners, and women. Under Roman law, all women—free or slave—were not permitted to sit with male citizens.

The Colosseum serves as an example of the Roman Empire at the height of its glory. Whether they sat with the patricians or the plebeians, citizens of Rome who attended the games could not help but be overwhelmed by the spectacle unfolding before them as well as the immense structure employed to stage the games. "It is . . . the most imposing of all ruins left by the classic world," Will Durant says of the Colosseum. "The Romans built like giants."[25]

## Gladiatorial Combat

During the games Romans could witness all manner of blood sports. In the mornings wild animals were set loose in the arena to fight against armed men or devour criminals or other undesirables, such as army deserters. Fights among female warriors were also common, as were sword battles featuring dwarfs.

The afternoons were set aside for serious gladiatorial combat. The typical gladiator was a slave captured in a foreign war. He was trained

*One of ancient Rome's most magnificent structures, the Colosseum (pictured), was built for blood sports and other forms of entertainment. The four-story, circular amphitheater could hold more than 50,000 spectators.*

## Flamma, Rome's Most Famous Gladiator

**A**lthough Hollywood depictions suggest that all gladiators fought to their deaths, that was not necessarily the case. Many gladiators survived their duels and lived to fight again. "There was hope, however slender," says John Percy Balsdon, professor of ancient history at Exeter College in England. "If the man survived his engagements in the arena, he might be discharged at the end of three years and set free at the end of five."[1]

Perhaps the most successful of all gladiators was Flamma, a Syrian who fought 34 times in the arena. Flamma was such a good fighter that he was offered his freedom four times but each time chose to remain a gladiator. Finally, Flamma did retire but did not live long to enjoy the fruits of freedom—he died at the age of 30.

He is buried in Sicily under a gravestone erected by a fellow gladiator, Delicatus. The gravestone reads: "Flamma, [armed gladiator], lived 30 years, fought 34 times, won 21 times, fought to a draw 9 times, defeated 4 times, a Syrian by nationality. Delicatus made this for his deserving comrade-in-arms."[2]

1. J.P.V.D. Balsdon, *Life and Leisure in Ancient Rome*. London: Phoenix, 2002, p. 289.
2. Quoted in Roman Empire & Colosseum, "Famous Gladiators," 2008. www.roman-colosseum.info.

in a school by veteran gladiators and expected to provide the spectacle of combat in the arena. (In Latin the term *gladiator* means "swordsman.") Gladiators learned to use swords, spears, shields, nets, and other weapons. Some specialized in fighting against wild animals such as lions or bears—these gladiators were known as the *bestiarii*. Says Durant, "Beasts fought men, men fought men; and the vast audience waited hopefully for the sight of death."[26]

Beneath the dirt floor of the arena, the Colosseum's builders constructed an intricate warren of rooms, cells, and cages. Slaves, gladiators, wild animals, criminals, and other unfortunate souls were kept prisoner beneath the arena floor, awaiting their turns to provide entertainment before the masses anxious to see their blood spilled. Says Balsdon, "You could have divided them into two classes: those who might hope to survive and those for whom there was no hope at all."[27]

The Romans were so enthralled by gladiatorial combat and other bloody events that authorities staged the games for 100 days or more a year. The emperors and other prominent and wealthy citizens sponsored the games, knowing they were vital for keeping the masses happy.

## The Heart of Rome

Outside the Colosseum, ancient Rome was a busy, bustling, and overcrowded city. It was also very noisy. The streets were paved with cobblestones; carts carrying food, fabrics, and other goods to the Roman markets bumped along the streets constantly. Even in an era 2,000 years before the arrival of motor vehicles, traffic was extremely congested as carts, horses, oxen, and pedestrians vied for space along the narrow streets of the city.

The Colosseum was only one of many impressive structures erected by the ancient Romans. If the Colosseum reflected Rome's love for entertainment and blood sports, the Forum represented the commercial and governmental heart of the empire. The Forum could be found in the valley between the Capitoline and Palatine Hills. Eventually, dozens of buildings, monuments, and statues were erected in the Forum. Among them were the Arch of Titus, a monument erected to celebrate Titus's conquest of Judea; the circular Temple of Romulus, a monument to Rome's first ruler; and the Temple of Vesta, a shrine regarded as one of the most sacred sites in the city. Says Barry Cunliffe:

The Forum was the heart of Rome. It was here that the commercial activities of the Empire centered, where the most sacred rituals of the state were performed, where the Senate and the Assembly met, and where the law courts were situated—it was, in short, the center of the world. Banquets, funerals, triumphs, moving orations, and bloody massacres were all enacted here. But it was above all a place of the people, senators and beggars alike.[28]

## Arches, Vaults, and Columns

The architecture of the buildings in the Forum as well as other important structures in Rome made widespread use of arches. The Romans found that arches could support heavy weights, allowing them to build structures of two or more stories. Indeed, the first three stories of the Colosseum are lined by weight-supporting arches.

The typical arch features two vertical supports called piers. Atop the piers, wedge-shaped stones curve inward to form an arc. The central stone in the arc is known as the keystone. Roman architects also employed vaults, which are essentially three-dimensional arches. Each vault features a curved or domed ceiling.

Roman architecture is also dominated by the use of columns, a building technique the Romans borrowed from the Greeks. Columns could support heavy weights such as roofs. Sometimes, columns were used simply for ornamental purposes, erected to celebrate military victories or to honor emperors and other heroes. Among the tallest ornamental columns in Rome are Trajan's Column, the Column of Marcus Aurelius, and, in the Forum, the 44-foot-tall (13.4m) Column of Phocas. All paid tribute to Roman emperors.

Builders made use of a number of materials, including marble and limestone. Greek builders were the first to mix lime, sand, and water to make mortar that was used to cement the stones together. The Romans took the Greeks' idea and made improvements. By using coarser grains of sand as well as mixing in small stones, the Romans developed a much stronger substance they employed to fashion bridges and similar structures. Today, that substance is known as concrete.

## Cold Plunges and Hot Baths

The architecture and building techniques of the Romans were spread throughout the city. Among the most common facilities found in Rome were the public baths—by the reign of Emperor Augustus, there were some 170 baths located in Rome.

A public bath was known as a *thermarum*. The baths were heated—in the first century BC, the Romans developed a method for heating the water by using hot air blown through a furnace. Each *thermarum* featured an *apodyterium*, which was the dressing room where patrons left their clothes to be watched over by servants or slaves. Other rooms included the *palaestra*, a gymnasium where they could exercise before bathing; the *frigidarium*, a room where patrons plunged first into a cold bath; the *tepidarium*, where they dried themselves following the cold plunge; and finally, the *caldarium*, which featured a steam room and hot bath.

*Spectators give the "thumbs down" signal that tells the victorious gladiator not to spare the life of his defeated opponent. Gladiatorial combat could be bloody and brutal—and the Romans loved it that way.*

The baths were extremely popular, with many people attending them daily or at least several times a week. The admission fee was minimal, and children bathed for free. Men and women bathed separately, either in separate rooms or during hours reserved for use by the separate genders. Surrounding the baths were gardens, exercise areas, and food stands. Says Balsdon, "Socially, the baths were important meeting—and mixing—places, and in a town everyone had his favorite baths, where he met his friends."[29]

## Life as a Patrician

The patricians—who could afford to build their own baths—were more likely to bathe at home. The typical homes of the patricians not only featured baths, attended to by slaves, but open-air courtyards that included ornate fountains. This area of the home was known as the atrium. The living quarters were built in a square, surrounding the courtyard and fountain. The house of a patrician was known as a *domus*. A patrician usually owned a *domus* in Rome as well as a country estate outside the city walls.

Inside the *domus* the patrician's family could enjoy their own bedrooms, a dining room, kitchen, lavatory, and library. The materials and workmanship used in the construction of the *domus* reflected the wealth of the inhabitants. In the homes of the wealthiest patricians, the faucets that fed the fountains in the atrium were often carved. These carvings depicted men, animals, or mythical creatures. Mosaic tiles were usually employed in the fountains; the mosaics formed images that often told stories that held some significance for the household—perhaps the owner's participation in an event of importance in Roman society. The mosaics also told stories of Roman history or myth.

Slaves maintained the household and cooked the meals. Patricians were served dinners with three courses: an appetizer of eggs, shellfish, or vegetables; an entrée of cooked meat and vegetables, and a dessert of fruit or pastry. When friends were invited over for a dinner party, the dishes may have included exotic selections such as ostrich or flamingo meat. During the meal, diners reclined around the table on couches, with the host occupying the center couch. The other guests were seated in order of importance, with the most socially prominent positioned nearest the host. To the class-conscious Romans, the seating order at the dinner party of a prominent aristocrat spoke volumes about each guest's status in Roman society. Regardless of everyone's social status, though, diners ate with their fingers.

The sons of patricians were educated at home by private tutors. The students' curricula usually included lessons in poetry, literature, history, geography, and languages. Since many patricians were active in Roman government, public speaking and law were taught as well. These skills were important because the sons of patricians were expected to replace their fathers in positions of influence one day. Patrician daughters were given far less education—they were expected to be married off while still teenagers.

## Life as a Plebeian

The sons of plebeians could expect far fewer opportunities. If their fathers were craftsmen, such as metalsmiths, ceramicists, or stone masons, they were taught the skills of the trade by their fathers. Other plebeians made their livings as bakers, farmers, or shop owners.

Most plebeians lived in modest apartments. Shop owners may have lived above their places of business. Craftspeople and other moderately successful plebeians may have been able to afford some luxuries, such as running water, but most were poor and could afford few amenities. Entire families, including grandparents, parents, and children, were usually crammed into one-room flats. Water had to be hauled in from outdoors. Public latrines were available outside. Fire was often a hazard because cooking was done indoors on open fires.

As for the typical plebeian meal, it was of far less quality and quantity than what could be found on the patrician dinner table. Meat was a luxury, available only when the family could afford it. For most plebeians, meals were composed of bread and porridge.

Many plebeians would often go hungry—a fact that was well known by the ruling class. It was not unusual for Roman emperors to provide free grain to the poor. Titus was among Rome's most benevolent emperors, often sponsoring grain giveaways to destitute plebeians. When fire swept through the city, destroying the homes of many plebeian citizens, Titus sold some of the palace furniture to raise money for the relief of fire victims. "His greatest fault was uncontrollable generosity," says Durant. "He counted that day lost on which he had not made someone happy with a gift."[30] Titus ruled for just two years, dying of fever at the age of 81. Says Durant, "All Rome mourned him."[31]

## Roman Theater

Despite their low stations in life, the plebeian craftspeople contributed to the culture of Rome as builders and artisans, filling their city with impressive statuary as well as murals and ceramics. The arts and literature were important components of ancient Roman culture. In 55 BC the Roman consul Pompey ordered construction of the city's first theater. At first, plays were staged featuring male slaves as actors, but as theater became more popular, professional actors emerged, and some became wealthy stars of the Roman stage.

Roman drama fell into two categories: *fabula palliata*, which were Roman translations of Greek plays, and *fabula togata*, which were written by Romans for Roman audiences. At first, Roman plays were usually performed as short comedic skits or as mime shows that also featured acrobats, jugglers, dancing girls, and magicians. By the third century BC, the plays had grown longer, telling full stories while weaving intricate plots.

The first of the important Roman playwrights was Gnaeus Naevius, who was born around 270 BC and died in 201 BC. Naevius was a veteran of the Punic Wars. His tragedy *The Trojan Horse* told the story of the siege of Troy. It was the first play performed in the theater constructed by Pompey.

It was comedy, though, that entranced most Roman audiences. The playwright Titus Maccius Plautus, who lived from around 254 to 184 BC, authored several slapstick comedies, such as *The Pot of Gold*,

*The Braggart Warrior*, and *The Comedy of Asses*. In most of Plautus's comedies, the slaves were smarter than their masters, lusty old men chased comely young women, and the villains all got what was coming to them. Another important writer of comic plays was Publius Terentius Afer, known more familiarly as Terence, who lived from around 195 to 159 BC. His comedies, which included such titles as *The Girl from Andros*, *The Mother-in-Law*, and *The Brothers*, were more sophisticated in nature, in which characters exchanged insults and wisecracks.

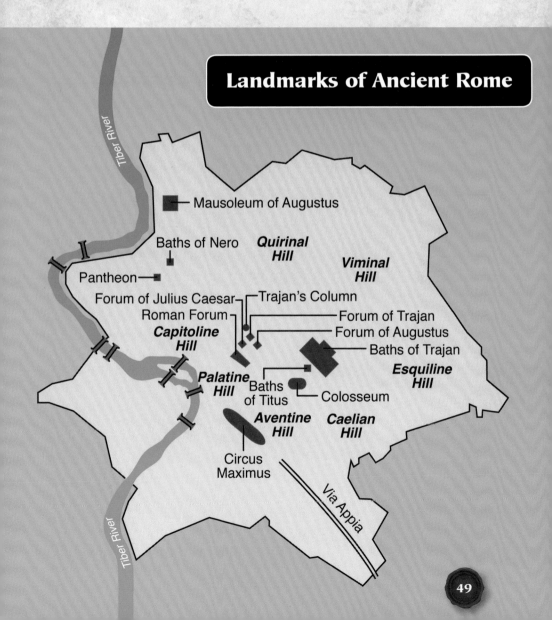

## Landmarks of Ancient Rome

Tiber River

Mausoleum of Augustus

Baths of Nero

*Quirinal Hill*

*Viminal Hill*

Pantheon

Forum of Julius Caesar

Trajan's Column

Roman Forum

Forum of Trajan

Forum of Augustus

*Capitoline Hill*

Baths of Trajan

*Palatine Hill*

Baths of Titus

Colosseum

*Esquiline Hill*

*Aventine Hill*

*Caelian Hill*

Circus Maximus

Via Appia

Tiber River

**O**ne of ancient Rome's most important shrines is the Temple of Vesta, built in the Forum to honor Vesta, goddess of hearth and home. Inside the temple a sacred fire was kept burning 24 hours a day, maintained by a group of priestesses known as the Vestal Virgins.

Six priestesses served as Vestal Virgins. They were chosen by the *pontifex maximus*, the high priest of Rome, from among the daughters of patricians. The priestesses could be as young as six. Once selected, they were expected to serve in the temple for at least 30 years, although most served for life. The priestesses lived in a house near the temple, known as the Hall of Vesta. They dressed entirely in white to emphasize their purity and were expected to remain virgins during the length of their service. If they were found to have violated their oath to remain chaste, the punishment was severe: burial alive while the male lover was beaten to death.

The Vestal Virgins did, however, enjoy many powers that were not granted to other Roman women. They were released from the authority of their fathers, invited to attend Roman festivals, and given seats of honor at the Colosseum. The Vestal Virgins also had the power to grant clemency to condemned criminals.

## Pagan Gods

Much of the art and culture of ancient Rome was produced in tribute to the Roman gods. For much of Rome's ancient history, the Romans were pagans—believing in multiple gods who represented the sun, seas, earth, sky, and other elements of nature. Romans hoped to please their gods, believing the gods held considerable influence over their daily lives. Among the gods were Neptune, god of the seas; Ceres, goddess of agriculture; Vesta, goddess of hearth and home; Mars, the god of war; Diana, the moon goddess; Juno, goddess of women and childbirth; and Minerva, goddess of healing and wisdom. The chief god was Jupiter. If a Roman farmer sought a good crop, he prayed to Ceres; if a child was ill, the parents prayed to Minerva.

Religious rituals were very important to Romans, who believed that if they prayed and followed the rituals closely, the gods would respond to their needs. They also believed that if a Roman neglected the rituals of prayer, the gods would grow angry and level punishment at the wayward soul. While praying to their gods, Romans often uttered the phrase "*Do ut des*," meaning "I give that you may give."

Personal sacrifice was an integral part of Roman prayer. During prayer Romans would make offerings to their gods, usually material possessions they donated to the temples of the gods. Wealthy Romans often erected statues, altars, or monuments as offerings to the gods. Gifts of gold, silver, or other precious metals were common. To decide on the size or value of their offerings, Romans generally responded to images in their dreams or consulted oracles—mystics who claimed to be in communication with the spirit world.

Animals were often sacrificed. Oxen, sheep, goats, pigs, and other livestock were led to the altar, where a priest slit the animal's throat. After the animal was slaughtered, the fat and bones were thrown into a fire built at the foot of the altar while the rest of the animal was consumed by the worshippers. Musicians were often hired to play during sacrificial ceremonies.

## Empire of Abundance

Roman art, architecture, and religious rituals were not confined to the city of Rome. As the Romans conquered other cities and their peoples, they spread their influence across their empire. As Rome spread its boundaries, Roman-style architecture emerged in many other cities in Europe as well as in the Middle East and Africa. In Spain, for example, visitors to the city of Mérida will find the ruins of a Roman-style amphitheater, a circus for chariot races, a forum for meetings of the People's

Assembly, a temple devoted to the goddess Diana, Roman-style bridges spanning the Guadiana and Albarregas Rivers, a Roman-style aqueduct, and an arch erected to honor the emperor Trajan.

The conquest of Carthage and other enemy states brought great wealth to Rome. Ships carrying marble, papyrus, spices, ivory, wine, oil, grains, precious metals, jewels, fabrics, and other booty from across the empire landed constantly at Italian seaports. The Romans were voracious consumers, importing most of their goods while exporting virtually nothing: The ships that sailed away from Italy were almost always empty, but they always returned with their holds stocked with goods. Each year, Romans consumed some 400,000 tons (362,874 metric tons) of grain, most of which was grown far from the Italian Peninsula.

Rome was an empire of abundance, but it was also a place where a relatively small number of patricians controlled the vast wealth of the empire while everyone else was either destitute or a slave. Indeed, it is believed that as many as a quarter of the people living under ancient Roman rule were slaves. Some wealthy Romans owned as many as 10,000 slaves.

## Spartacus and the Slave Revolt

The lives of slaves were spent in dismal toil; slave revolts were common. One of the most famous of the slave revolts erupted in 73 BC. Seventy-eight slaves trained at a school for gladiators in the city of Capua, about 175 miles (282km) south of Rome, escaped and were able to arm themselves. At first the former gladiators were merely interested in gaining their freedom, but as word of their escape spread, other slaves fled their masters and joined their movement. To lead them they chose Spartacus, formerly of the Greek region known as Thrace. Eventually, the ranks of the slave army grew to some 120,000 men. Spartacus led his slave army south, hoping to fight his way out of Italy and escape across the Mediterranean.

Along the way the slaves looted Italian cities, killing freeborn citizens, setting fires, and inflicting other forms of mayhem. Back in Rome the slave-owning aristocrats were horrified by the uprising and found themselves living in fear, wondering whether their household slaves would rise against them and join the revolt. They demanded the Roman Senate take action and put down the uprising.

The Senate responded by sending Roman legions to halt the advance of the slave army, but the soldiers met with mixed results, winning some confrontations with the slaves but losing many as well. Legions were hastily recalled from Spain to help swell the ranks of the Roman army. The decisive battle was fought in 71 BC at Reggio Calabria, a city at the tip of the Italian Peninsula. Spartacus was killed in battle; most of his followers fled into the countryside. Some 6,000 slaves who were captured were crucified along the road known as the Appian Way, which connects Capua to Rome. Says Durant, "Their rotting bodies were left to hang for months, so that all masters might take comfort, and all slaves take heed."[32]

The beggars, craftspeople, laborers, and other ordinary Romans were just slightly better off than the slaves. They may have been free citizens of the empire, but they lived in poverty. Most found release and joy only at the Colosseum and other arenas where their attention was concentrated on the blood sports unfolding before them, rather than on the true problems festering below the surface of Roman society.

# Chapter 4

# Rome's Slow Decline

**M**ost Romans paid heed to the mystics and soothsayers of the era, who told fortunes and read omens to help guide people through their daily lives. Among these seers were the sibyls: prophetesses who spoke in frenzied tongues, often making bizarre predictions.

The predictions by the sibyls were compiled into a collection of books, published between the second century BC and the third century AD, known as *The Sibylline Oracles*. The sibyls portended dark days ahead for the Roman Empire. Among the warnings uttered by the sibyls were these words:

> On thee some day shall come, O haughty Rome,
>
> A fitting stroke from heaven, and thou the first
>
> Shalt bend to the neck, be leveled to the earth,
>
> And fire shall utterly consume thee, beat
>
> Upon thy pavements, and thy wealth shall perish.[33]

The predictions by the sibyls would largely come true. It would take several centuries, but the Roman Empire would not endure. Plagued by internal strife, often ruled by madmen and tyrants, unable to control a large and unwieldy domain, Rome was slowly but surely decaying from within. Eventually in this weakened state, it would fall prey to a steadily increasing onslaught of invaders from the east whom historians labeled the barbarians.

# Caesar's Power Grab

The roots of decline started growing during some of Rome's most glorious days. As Roman patricians gained wealth and power, they sought to control the empire as absolute rulers—much in contrast to the ideals envisioned by the founders of the republic who rebelled against the Etruscan kings. The first of Rome's absolute rulers was Julius Caesar.

In 49 BC, as Caesar returned to Rome following his campaign against the Gauls, the Roman Senate feared Caesar would use his army to attack his rival, the general Gnaeus Pompeius Magnus, known familiarly as Pompey. To avoid civil war, the Senate ordered Caesar to disband his army. Caesar refused. He knew this would be his moment of triumph. Instead, Caesar led his army in an attack on Rome. As his army crossed the Rubicon River on its approach to Rome, Caesar is said to have declared, "Let the dice fly high!"[34] Caesar used a gambling term because he was sure his ploy for power represented a high-stakes gamble.

As it turned out, Caesar's daring grab for power was not much of a gamble—his army encountered little resistance. He marched into the city and declared himself dictator, finding a once-defiant Senate now willing to bow down to his authoritarian power. Indeed, the Roman senators elected Caesar dictator for life.

Caesar used his new powers to eliminate Pompey, plunging Rome into four years of civil war. Caesar emerged victorious and pledged to rebuild the state. He did bring many reforms and benefits to the Roman people. For instance, he distributed land to the veterans of his army in payment for their service and enacted a partial abolishment of slavery.

He expanded Roman colonies across Europe; in Egypt he used the Roman army to eliminate the enemies of the queen, Cleopatra, establishing her as sole ruler. Caesar also romanced the queen, producing a son and sparking a scandal back in Rome.

# The Death of Caesar

Returning from his adventures in Egypt, Caesar devoted a large portion of the Roman treasury to erecting new buildings in the capital

# Destruction of Pompeii

The fire that swept through Rome during Nero's reign was not the only catastrophe to strike the empire. About 175 miles (282km) south of Rome, the city of Pompeii was destroyed virtually within hours when it was engulfed in lava and rock spewed by the nearby volcano Mount Vesuvius.

A city of some 20,000 people, Pompeii was a commercial center where grains, wool, olive oil, and wines were sold, making many citizens wealthy. But on August 24 in AD 79, the citizens of Pompeii suddenly saw black smoke rising from Mount Vesuvius.

The destruction was swift. Lava poured down the mountainside. The volcano also sent dust and rock high into the air, and these rained down on Pompeii. Some of the rock was on fire as it crashed through the roofs of people's homes and shops. Many panicked citizens who ran through the streets choked to death on the thick dust falling from the sky.

Meanwhile, a heavy rain started falling. Rather than extinguish the fires, the rain only added to people's misery—it caused a heavy torrent of mud and stone to cascade down the mountain and crash into people's homes. Parts of Pompeii would eventually be buried under 8 feet (2.4m) or more of mud and volcanic ash. Centuries later, archaeologists uncovered the bodies of the dead, their corpses eerily preserved by the ash that formed hard casts around them.

After three days, the lava stopped flowing. When the skies cleared of dust and smoke, only the rooftops of Pompeii were visible.

city. Caesar placed himself at the head of all Roman courts and personally presided over several major cases. To encourage childbirth, Caesar awarded tracts of land to fathers who produced at least three children.

But Caesar had little use for the Senate or the People's Assembly. He stocked the Senate with his cronies, who could be expected to adopt the laws he wanted without opposition. He ignored the tribunes, who were supposed to be protecting the rights of the plebeians. Although never officially declared emperor of Rome, Caesar was Rome's absolute ruler. Most rulers who followed Caesar also found little use for the Roman Senate and assemblies. Rome was now a republic in name only—the true power would be concentrated in the hands of the type of absolute monarchs the founders of the republic thought they had outlawed 500 years earlier. "Do you see the kind of man into whose hands the state has fallen?" lamented the great Roman orator Cicero in a letter to a friend. "It pains me to think of the mistakes and wrongs of ours that are responsible for this."[35]

Caesar's rule lasted just five years. As Caesar consolidated his power, many of his foes seethed over the widespread changes in Roman life. They were particularly angry at the dictator's decision to grant full Roman citizenship to freed slaves—giving them the same rights as freeborn citizens.

Caesar also led campaigns to stamp out corruption, angering many entrenched politicians and others who owed their lucrative posts to a corrupt system. Elections for Senate and other posts were notoriously corrupt; many Roman citizens were more than willing to sell their votes. Meanwhile, Caesar made plans to expand the Roman Empire into new territories—he proposed an expedition to conquer Germany. Fearing this conquest would make Caesar even more powerful and popular among the Roman people, a group of aristocrats hatched a plan, and on March 15 in 44 BC they moved against him. Surrounding Caesar in the Forum, the conspirators drew their knives and ended the life of the dictator.

# The Revered One

Following the death of Caesar, Rome was again plunged into chaos and civil war. Rising from this turmoil was Caesar's nephew and adopted son, Gaius Octavius.

Octavius had been studying in Greece when he received news of his father's murder. Just 19 years old, Octavius hurried back to Rome and raised an army among Caesar's former supporters. In the months following Caesar's assassination, the military leader Marcus Antonius—known more familiarly as Mark Antony—had attempted to seize power in Rome. After Octavius's return, Antony formed an uneasy alliance with Caesar's son as well as a third leader, Roman general Marcus Lepidus. But Antony eventually pushed Lepidus aside and then turned against Octavius.

Antony had entered into an alliance (and love affair) with Cleopatra. Together, the two challenged Octavius, but in a naval battle in 31 BC near the Greek city of Actium, Octavius's forces prevailed, routing Antony's men and forcing Antony and Cleopatra to flee back to Egypt. As Octavius closed in, Antony committed suicide by falling on his sword. Cleopatra also took her own life—she is believed to have consumed poison, although popular myth has long suggested Cleopatra pressed a poisonous snake to her breast.

Octavius was now 32 years old. He returned to Rome intent on consolidating his authority, thus rendering the Senate and People's Assembly even more powerless than ever. In fact, Octavius transferred all the powers of the tribunes to himself, taking over the responsibilities of looking after the rights of the plebeians. The Roman people, weary of years of civil war, were willing to cede power to a single, authoritative individual who would end the turmoil. At first, the Roman Senate elected him consul, but in time his power would grow so absolute that the Senate rarely questioned his word. In 27 BC the Senate granted Octavius unlimited authority, conferring on him the title Augustus, which means "revered one." The Senate's action effectively made Augustus the first emperor of Rome. Under Augustus, the army took an oath of allegiance to the emperor—not to the Senate or the people of Rome.

*A fifteenth-century painter depicts the popular version of the deaths of Antony and Cleopatra after their failed attempt to seize control of Rome: Antony kills himself with his sword and Cleopatra presses poisonous snakes to her breasts.*

## Rome's Golden Age

As emperor, Augustus rebuilt much of Rome that had fallen into disrepair in the years of civil war—under his authority, he rebuilt 82 religious temples. He also authorized construction of the Theater of Marcellus, the Temple of Apollo, and the Horologium, a huge public sundial. Rome's public water system was also modernized under Augustus.

As emperor, Augustus further expanded Rome's boundaries, bringing prosperity to the empire. Following his conquest of Egypt in 30 BC, Augustus personally led an army on a campaign through Spain in 26 BC. Later, he extended Roman rule into the Balkans and Germany. All of these forays brought more wealth home to Rome. The reign of Augustus marked the beginning of the era of the *Pax Romana* (Roman Peace)—the golden age of Rome.

Under Augustus the empire expanded, but it was becoming increasingly clear that the army was having trouble controlling Rome's vast and distant realm. Roman soldiers found themselves putting down rebellions in Britain and Judea. By the second century AD, Roman outposts were constantly under attack by barbarians and others who decided they had endured Roman rule for too long.

## The Scheming Sejanus

Augustus died in AD 14. He had hoped to be succeeded by either of his grandsons, Gaius or Lucius, but they had preceded him in death. They may have been murdered by Augustus's wife, Livia, who wanted her son Tiberius to inherit the throne. (Tiberius was not Augustus's son—Livia had been wed once before she married the future emperor.) Without his favorite grandsons available to succeed him, Augustus reluctantly accepted Tiberius as his heir. When he formalized the succession by adopting Tiberius, Augustus declared, "This I do for reasons of state."[36] And as he lay dying, knowing that Tiberius would succeed him, Augustus feared Tiberius would lead Rome into disaster. On his death bed, the old emperor is said to have uttered, "Alas for the Roman people, to be ground by jaws that crunch so slowly!"[37]

Augustus had good reason to fear for the future of Rome. He had maintained cordial relations with the Senate; although he held absolute power, he relied on the Senate for advice. At first, Tiberius maintained similar relations with the Senate, but soon virtually ignored Rome's legislative body. Moreover, Tiberius soon lost interest in governing, turning over the administration of the empire to a close aide and leader of the palace guards, Lucius Aelius Sejanus. As for Tiberius, he retired to the Mediterranean island of Capri. He was now 67 years old and had no intentions of returning to Rome.

Sejanus turned out to be a cruel and despotic individual. "He advanced his fortune by selling offices to the highest bidders," says Will Durant. "A senate of real Romans would soon have overthrown him; but the senate had, with many exceptions, become a . . . club too listless to wield competently even the [minimal] authority that Tiberius urged it to retain."[38]

The scheming Sejanus's real intention was to seize power for himself—he engineered the murder of Tiberius's son and heir, Drusus, and exiled other members of the emperor's family in order to get them out of the way as he prepared for his own rise to power. But Sejanus went too far. His plans for the assassination of the emperor found their way to Capri and the ears of Tiberius. When the emperor learned that Sejanus intended to have him assassinated, he ordered his former aide arrested and executed. Tiberius also ordered Sejanus's friends and family members, many of them innocent, put to death as well. Tiberius intended to ensure that all remnants of Sejanus's plot were wiped out.

## Caligula and Nero

Internal strife continued to plague the empire. Tiberius may have escaped assassination, but other rulers were not as fortunate. Assassination of emperors turned out to be a common method employed by their enemies to achieve power. In one 23-year period, 30 different emperors would rule Rome. Among these were the so-called barracks emperors—military rulers who managed to muster power for short periods until their armies were pushed aside by other leaders able to assemble even larger armies.

Some emperors were simply insane. Caligula treated his horse to a life of luxury and suggested he would make the animal a consul of Rome. He spent lavishly and foolishly, soon depleting the palace treasury, then imposed new taxes to restore his personal coffers. When Caligula declared himself a god, his enemies—convinced the emperor was insane—orchestrated his assassination.

Also of dubious sanity was Nero, who ascended to the throne at the age of 16. Dominated by his mother, Agrippina, Nero seethed under her control and, when he could endure her meddling no longer, ordered her murder. Otherwise, Nero fancied himself an actor, often taking roles in plays. His fondness for the stage horrified Rome's aristocrats, who believed acting a profession well below the dignity of an emperor.

In AD 64 fire swept through the city, destroying a third of Rome and leaving half the population homeless. In the face of such despair, Nero ordered the erection of a lavish palace featuring sprawling gardens as well as a private lake and zoo. When rumors circulated that Nero had ordered the fire ignited to clear room for his new palace, the emperor panicked and searched for a scapegoat. He decided to persecute a small and obscure religious cult that had recently settled in Rome: the Christians. Accusing the Christians of setting the fire, he ordered them arrested and had hundreds tortured and killed for sport in the arena.

Nero's lavish spending and disregard for the rights of his citizens continued. Finally, in AD 68 even the ordinarily impotent Senate could endure his antics no more. Mustering courage it had not found in many decades, the Senate declared Nero a public enemy and ordered his arrest and execution. With his enemies closing in, Nero took his own life. His final words are said to have been, "What an artist the world is losing!"[39]

## Christianity Arrives in Rome

The persecution of the Christians did not end with the death of Nero. Since the death of Jesus, the Romans had long harbored suspicions about the followers of this new faith. The term *Christian* was at first used derisively in the Roman-dominated city of Antioch in Syria to describe members of this new and strange cult.

The Romans concocted many myths about the Christians, including that they were cannibals and engaged in incest. Gaius Plinus Caecilius Secundus, known more familiarly as Pliny the Younger, served as an aide to Emperor Trajan, who came to power 30 years after Nero's

The emperor Nero is rumored to have ordered a fire set to make room for a lavish new palace. The fire burned a third of Rome and left half of the city's population homeless. A movie poster depicts the uncaring emperor singing while his city burns.

death. Pliny had several Christians arrested and tortured, and he was unnerved by their stubbornness and grim refusal to renounce their beliefs, even under the threat of death. He advised Trajan that the Christians represented a threat to the empire because of their "depraved and excessive superstition."[40] Trajan noted that while the Christians may have been a strange people, he hardly found them threatening. He found no reason to have Christians rounded up and executed.

As the Christians arrived in Rome, the new religion found favor particularly among Roman women, who had few rights of citizenship in the capital city. Women were attracted to Christianity because it promised them spiritual equality. The rite of accepting communion, for example, could be practiced alongside men.

Rome had always been a pluralistic society, willing to accept other gods, but at first Romans found it hard to accept Christianity because Christians refused to make the sacrifices that the pagan faiths required, nor would Christians accept pagan gods alongside Jesus. However, in time ordinary Romans found themselves attracted to Christianity since the faith denounced the rich and praised the meek and poor. This was an important distinction; for centuries Roman society had been dominated by a handful of wealthy aristocrats while the vast majority of the population lived in terrible poverty.

## The Christians Turn to Martyrdom

Other emperors were not as easygoing as Trajan when it came to dealing with the Christians. The third-century AD Christian author Quintus Tertullianus wrote that Emperor Domitian, who reigned from AD 81 to 96, "almost equaled Nero in cruelty"[41] in his treatment of Christians.

Under Emperor Gordianus III, who reigned from AD 238 to 244, groups of thugs known as the *vicomagistri* were appointed to hunt down Christians and arrest or abuse them. (The term comes from the Latin word *vicus*, which means "neighborhood"—essentially, each neighborhood had its Christian-hating roughnecks.) The formerly pluralistic Roman society was now firmly tyrannical and intolerant.

# The Ordeal of Blandina

As the emperors of Rome initiated persecutions against the Christians, many turned to martyrdom—they elected to die rather than renounce their faith. Of the many martyrs who died during the Roman persecutions, the story of Blandina provided many Christians with the strength to endure the tortures inflicted on them.

Blandina was a 15-year-old Christian slave girl who lived in the Gallic city of Lyons. Under Roman rule in the year AD 177, the Roman governor ordered a roundup of Christians to provide entertainment for a Roman festival. At first, Blandina and other Christians were imprisoned and tortured; often their flesh was burned with hot coals or irons. Despite the tortures, Blandina refused to renounce her faith. "I am a Christian and we commit no wrongdoing," she insisted. The Christians who survived the tortures were taken to an amphitheater, where they were tossed into the arena to be devoured by wild beasts. Blandina was tied to a stake, but while other Christians were attacked by the animals, the beasts spared Blandina's life.

She was taken back to prison but later returned to the arena along with other prisoners. Again, the animals killed the others first—only Blandina remained alive. Finally, the Romans sent a steer into the arena. The steer attacked Blandina, tossing her into the air with its horns. A guard then finished off the girl with a dagger.

Blandina was later granted sainthood by the Catholic Church. Today, the ruins of the amphitheater in Lyons have been preserved, including the stake where Blandina is said to have been bound during her ordeal.

Quoted in Judith Couchman, *The Mystery of the Cross: Bringing Ancient Christian Images to Life.* Downers Grove, IL: InterVarsity, 2009, p. 65.

In AD 303 Emperor Diocletian burned churches and scriptures while torturing and imprisoning Christians, vowing to wipe out the religion once and for all. Many Christians faced their abuses and tortures with quiet and relentless resolve, believing their martyrdom would prove their faith and preserve Christianity. Says University of Virginia historian Robert Louis Wilken, "Like ancient Rome, the new Christian Rome has its founding heroes, but they were martyrs, not military heroes, and they vanquish their foes not by strength of arms but by faith in Christ."[42] The Christians would eventually win acceptance in the Roman Empire: around AD 312, the emperor Constantine converted to Christianity.

## Dividing the Empire

As the Christians turned to martyrdom, the Roman emperors realized that the Christians were not the only threat to the future of the empire. Indeed, while the emperors dealt with internal strife, they were forced to defend Rome's receding borders. To maintain order, Diocletian divided the empire into four sections, appointing rulers, each with the title "caesar" to oversee their portions of the domain. To administer his portion of the empire, Diocletian moved the capital to the Asian city of Nicomedia. (Today, the city is known as Izmit in modern-day Turkey.) Other caesars maintained their capitals away from Rome as well: the city of Rome was no longer the capital of the Roman Empire.

Diocletian's reorganization of the empire helped stave off the inevitable, but other emperors were forced to deal with emboldened invaders. Even before Diocletian's rule, Emperor Valerian found himself suing for peace during a campaign against the Persians. When Valerian arrived in Iraq, the Persian king Shapur made him kneel down before his conqueror, then took him prisoner. Shapur had Valerian enslaved and later flayed, displaying his skin in a Persian temple.

The defeat and imprisonment of Valerian is regarded as one of Rome's most humiliating defeats. Says Durant, "Under the force of these blows, and the disorderly elevation and assassination of emperors by troops, the imperial prestige collapsed. [The emperors] lost their hold upon Rome's enemies, even upon her subjects and citizens. Revolts broke out everywhere."[43]

## Romulus, the Last Emperor

The worst was yet to come. In AD 410 the Visigoth leader Alaric sacked the city of Rome. He encountered little resistance. In the years following Alaric's victory, the rulers of the eastern portion of the empire dispensed with Roman customs and culture, marking the birth of what would become the Byzantine Empire, which endured into the fifteenth century.

In the western portion of the empire, local nobles stopped paying their taxes to the Romans and instead made peace with the peoples of France, Germany, and other northern European regions—all of whom were known to the Romans as "barbarians." For centuries, there would be little central government throughout Europe, and instead feudal barons controlled their own estates and the people who lived on them. This era represented the birth of medieval Europe.

Ironically, the final Roman emperor was named Romulus. He ascended to the throne as a teenager and remained in power for less than a year, abdicating as a Germanic monarch, Odoacer, declared himself king of Italy in AD 476. Romulus lived out the rest of his life in peaceful obscurity. With his abdication, the Roman Empire in the west came to an end.

# Chapter 5

# What Is the Legacy of Ancient Rome?

For all the troubles that plagued Rome, the city was founded on the basic principle that all peoples would be welcomed within its borders. Africans, Indians, Gauls, Germans—all were invited to live in the city and become Romans. The Romans respected cultural diversity. In Latin, the Roman language, this unification of all peoples into one nation is summed up with the words *E pluribus unum*, which means "Out of many, one."

Centuries after the fall of Rome, the American founders took great inspiration from that concept and adopted *E pluribus unum* as the motto of their new nation. That motto can be found on the Great Seal of the United States. Moreover, it is found on American currency, serving as a daily reminder to all citizens that America is a nation of immigrants who have come together to form one people. Says Steven Bonta, "The fall of Rome, although a tragedy to the generations that experienced it, has proven to be a blessing for mankind in the longer term. For while Rome's collapse led to a dark age of several centuries, it also made possible, in the longer run, the rise of a modern civilization that has far eclipsed Rome's greatest achievements."[44]

## Branches of Government

As young students, John Adams, Thomas Jefferson, James Madison, and the other framers of American democracy all read the published histories of the Roman republic, finding inspiration in Rome's form of representative government. Years later, as they drafted the US

Constitution, the founders picked the best features of the Roman republic and applied them to American law.

They were impressed with the balance of power achieved during the Roman republic, with the Senate, tribunes, and consuls sharing in the administration of the government. From that notion, the founders created an executive branch as well as a legislative branch that includes the US Senate and US House of Representatives. The Senate was conceived as an upper house, much as the Roman Senate was regarded: a body with limited legislative powers but considerable influence over foreign policy. In Rome the senators enjoyed long terms—in fact, they served for life. In America the founders recognized the importance of stability in the upper house but drew the line at lifetime terms—instead, they decided senators could serve for terms of six years.

The House would be the lower chamber, patterned after the People's Assembly. Tribunes served for short terms—one year in ancient Rome—and conceived most legislation because they were considered closest to the electorate. Under the American Constitution, US representatives can serve for terms of two years and are also responsible for writing most legislation.

The consuls served as the executives, much as the president serves as chief executive of the United States, given authority to carry out the daily functions of government. The consuls were also the commanders in chief of the military, just as the US president serves in that role. Says Bonta, "Like America, early Rome placed great importance on separating and limiting the powers of government."[45]

The framers of the US Constitution were also aware of the veto power held by the consuls over legislation adopted by Roman legislators, adding another degree to the balance of power. *Veto* is a Latin word that means "I forbid." In the US Constitution, the president is provided with veto powers over actions by Congress.

## The Example of Cincinnatus

The framers of the US Constitution were also impressed with the Roman concept that ordinary citizens could be summoned to answer the

## A Modern Gladiatorial Contest

**P**layed at Cowboys Stadium in Arlington, Texas, the 2011 Super Bowl was the forty-fifth version of the National Football League (NFL) championship game since the merger of the NFL with the old American Football League in the 1960s. Officially, the 2011 game was designated Super Bowl XLV.

The NFL has used Roman numerals to identify its championship game since 1971, when the event was officially designated Super Bowl V. (Prior to 1970 the game was not even known as the Super Bowl—it was officially known as the AFL-NFL Championship Game.) When the decision was made to use Roman numerals, the league applied the standard retroactively to the prior 4 games—they became Super Bowls I, II, III, and IV.

The idea of using Roman numerals to identify the league's championship game was concocted by the NFL's former commissioner Pete Rozelle, who felt the game reflected a modern gladiatorial contest—the strongest men in America would compete in America's grandest coliseums. Says Clark Haptonstall, an associate professor of sports management at Rice University, "Rozelle felt by using Roman numerals it kind of gave that gladiator-type Roman feel. It was something that differentiated the Super Bowl from other sporting events."

Quoted in Jeffrey Fekete, *Making the Big Game: Tales of an Accidental Spectator*. Minneapolis: Two Harbors, 2009, p. 2.

call to duty. They were particularly drawn to the story of Lucius Quinctius Cincinnatus, a farmer who, during a crisis in the year 458 BC, agreed to serve as consul and dictator.

Just some 50 years after the ouster of the Etruscan kings, Rome was still vulnerable to its enemies. In this case Rome was threatened by the

Aequi, a tribe based in the nearby Apennine Mountains whose attacks on Roman merchants threatened the city's trade.

The Senate made provisions for such situations, establishing the position of dictator because, the Senate believed, in times of crisis a powerful leader should be installed and provided with authoritarian powers. Following the crisis, the dictator was expected to step down. In fact, the Senate placed a sunset provision on the dictator's powers—limiting the dictator's time in office to six months.

To serve as Rome's first dictator, the Senate summoned Cincinnatus. He assumed command of the army and met the Aequi in battle at Algidus Mons, a mountain about 12 miles (19km) southeast of Rome. The battle was brief and resulted in a Roman victory. Following the battle, Cincinnatus relinquished his powers and returned to his farm. He had served as dictator for a mere 16 days.

Years later, the founding fathers envisioned the role of the president and members of Congress in a similar fashion—that citizens would put aside their private lives for brief periods so that they may serve the needs of their country. Many historians have compared George Washington with Cincinnatus—a farmer who left his fields in Virginia to lead the Continental army and later serve as the first American president. (The British poet Lord Byron even called Washington "the Cincinnatus of the West."[46]) Washington helped foster this comparison when, in a message to Congress, he said, "I have no lust for power but wish with as much fervency as any Man upon this wide extended Continent for an opportunity of turning the Sword into a plow share."[47]

As for Cincinnatus, a statue of the Roman stands at Sawyer Point in Cincinnati, Ohio, a city that was indirectly named in honor of the Roman hero. (The city was actually named for the Society of Cincinnati, an historical group named after the farmer-dictator.) The statue depicts Cincinnatus holding a wooden ax handle in one hand, symbolizing his power as Roman leader, while his other hand rests on a plow, a symbol of his private life.

## Under Roman Law

Service to one's country may also be found in the form of military duty. In ancient Rome male citizens were expected to serve in the Roman legions. It was regarded as a duty of Roman citizenship. Centuries later, America and other democratic nations instituted citizen militias and later military drafts, calling citizens to active duty as the need arose. Eventually, Rome turned to a professional army. Today, America and other nations also rely on full-time professional soldiers.

In addition to establishing a republican form of government and a precedent for citizen involvement in the government and the military, the Romans established the concept that all citizens were equal under the law and all had to obey the law. Many of today's laws are based on laws established by Roman leaders. Julius Caesar established laws against the charging of prohibitively high interest rates on loans—similar laws are on the books today in America. Caesar also established a process that enabled many Roman citizens to escape their debts by allowing them to declare bankruptcy. Today, modern bankruptcy laws closely resemble the policies established by Caesar. Says British writer and historian Michael Grant:

It is worth remembering that the entire world of order, in which we live, is the creation of the ancients, and in particular the Romans. It is true that the law of our land, as we know it today, is not Roman law. Nevertheless, it was the Romans . . . who concluded that we ought to live within a legal framework. And that is what we do. In other words, we live our lives through the grace of Roman law. So we owe it to the Roman lawyers . . . that we live in comparative peace and orderliness. Without Roman law, we should merely be in the jungle.[48]

## Dictatorships Endure

Caesar and other Roman leaders established the concept of law and order, but they also instituted a much darker legacy that is often felt in the world today. In the years before Caesar crossed the Rubicon River to seize power, Rome was occasionally led by dictators like Cincinnatus who served briefly and then voluntarily relinquished their powers. But when Caesar bullied the Senate into naming him dictator for life, he set a precedent that would be followed by many other unscrupulous and evil leaders whose dictatorial authority resulted in horrific consequences for their countries and other countries as well.

The French dictator Napoléon Bonaparte often compared himself with Julius Caesar, envisioning France as the center of a new European empire, to be modeled on the Roman Empire forged by Caesar. By 1799 Napoléon was France's most powerful general. That year he staged a coup, seizing power from the French Directory, a panel that

*Following in the footsteps of the Roman emperors, Adolf Hitler of Germany (left) and Benito Mussolini of Italy (right) gained authority during times of crisis and then found ways to seize absolute power. Mussolini sought to create a second golden age of Rome.*

administered the government of France. At the time, Napoleon likened his actions to those of Caesar when the Roman crossed the Rubicon, seizing power from the Roman Senate. Moreover, Napoleon declared himself "first consul for life," just as Caesar had himself declared dictator for life. Later, Napoleon took the title of emperor.

In the twentieth century, the dictatorships of Benito Mussolini in Italy, Francisco Franco in Spain, Joseph Stalin in the Soviet Union, and Adolf Hitler in Germany would plunge their countries into wars and internal purges, costing tens of millions of lives. Each attained power by gaining authority during times of crisis—just as the Roman dictators had centuries before—then finding ways to seize absolute power.

Mussolini was enthralled with the notion of ascending to power in the style of the ancient Roman dictators. As an Italian, Mussolini strove to link his Fascist regime to the grandeur of ancient Rome. He ordered the preservation of ruins and restored many of the temples and other buildings from the ancient age. He often staged public events amid the Roman ruins, particularly those in the Forum. Unlike Napoléon, whose hero was Julius Caesar, Mussolini regarded Augustus with much more respect and awe. It was Augustus who had greatly expanded the borders of the Roman Empire; Mussolini aimed for modern Italy to be a conquering nation as well. And so, shortly after he ascended to power in 1922, Mussolini declared a new *Pax Romana*—a second golden age of Rome.

Three years later Mussolini made his intentions clear in a speech titled "The New Rome." He said, "My ideas are clear, my orders exact, and certain to become a reality. Within five years, Rome must strike all the nations of the world as a source of wonder: huge, well organized, powerful, as it was at the time of the Augustan empire."[49] In 1936, after years of preparing the Italian army for combat, Mussolini embarked on an invasion of Ethiopia in North Africa—a replay, perhaps, of the Punic Wars of centuries before when the ancient Romans conquered Carthage.

The dictatorships of Mussolini and Hitler ended with the defeat of the Axis Powers in World War II, but the war did not end dictatorship as a mode of governance. Dictators have remained in power into the

# The Deterioration of Rome's Ancient Ruins

The ancient Romans left the modern world proof of their culture: the impressive ruins of the Colosseum, Forum, and other grand structures. However, in recent years many of those structures have sustained damage. In 2009 a ceiling collapsed in the ruins of Nero's Golden Palace. In 2010 the ruins of Pompeii suffered a number of collapses—destroyed were the remnants of a house where gladiators prepared for battle as well as a structure known as the House of Chaste Lovers. Also in 2010 several chunks of the Colosseum broke free. Many of the ruins on the Palatine, which includes the palatial homes of emperors and aristocrats, are showing cracks.

Critics contend that the Italian government does not devote enough resources to maintaining the ancient ruins. "We're stunned when some walls fall down," says archaeologist Andrea Carandini, "but these are ruins not systematically maintained, so that the miracle is that so few of them collapse."[1]

Italian authorities devote 0.2 percent of the national budget to preserving the country's ancient ruins. In contrast, the French government devotes 1 percent of its national budget to preserving ancient ruins and artifacts. Roberto Cecchi, undersecretary of the Italian Cultural Ministry, conceded that there is no overall plan to maintain the ruins—most are repaired on an as-needed basis.

Other culprits are believed to be tourists—some 3 million a year traipse through the ruins of Pompeii. "Having millions of visitors just stamping around Pompeii or Venice each year causes its own destruction,"[2] says archaeologist Clementina Panella.

1. Quoted in Frances D'Emilio, Associated Press, "The Fall of the Roman Empire, Round 2," *Philadelphia Inquirer*, November 12, 2010, p. A2.
2. Quoted in Michael Day, "Down Pompeii? The Ruin of Italy's Cultural Heritage," *Independent* (London), December 4, 2010. www.independent.co.uk.

twenty-first century: Such modern-day dictators as Robert Mugabe of Zimbabwe and Kim Jong-Il of North Korea owe their styles of governance in no small part to the example set by Julius Caesar. In fact, a term for monarch or extreme ruler is the word *czar*, sometimes spelled *tsar*, which is derived from the name *Caesar*.

## Keeping Latin Alive

Those English words emerged from Latin roots. Latin was the language of ancient Rome, and although it is no longer spoken conversationally in Italy or anywhere else, it remains an important component of human communication. Many words in English and other contemporary languages, including Spanish, Italian, and French, have incorporated elements of Latin.

Moreover, Latin is employed in medical, scientific, and legal contexts. In American law habeas corpus is a protection against illegal imprisonment. A writ of habeas corpus requires a police agency to bring a defendant before a judge. In Latin the term means "you have the body." Another common Latin term used in American law is *certiorari*. The term's literal Latin translation is "to be informed." In American courts a writ of certiorari is filed by a losing party in a case. The writ asks a higher court, often the US Supreme Court, to accept the case on appeal.

While Latin is used frequently in American courts, it is the Roman Catholic Church, more than any other institution, that has kept Latin alive—an ironic truth, inasmuch as Christians were among those most persecuted during ancient Roman times. Today some Catholic services are conducted entirely in Latin.

Otherwise, Latin is often spoken in American high schools where the language is taught, usually as an elective. There are 1,200 chapters of the National Junior Classical League headquartered in high schools, and they include some 50,000 members. Activities sponsored by the league are "quiz bowl" competitions known as Certamen as well as a weeklong convention, held each summer at an American university, that some 1,500 high school Latin students attend. Each year, Latin students vie for a number of scholarships made available by the league that can total as much as $2,000.

As students research topics for term papers, they will often find Latin phrases used in the footnotes and endnotes of books and other source materials. Among the most common phrases are *ibid.* and *op. cit.* Short for *ibidem*, *ibid.* means the reference is the same as the previous citation, and *op. cit.*, short for *opus citatum*, means the reference has been cited previously in the notes.

# Leap Years, Big Ben, and the Super Bowl

The influence of the Romans can be found not only in American law and literature but in American architecture as well. Roman-style architecture has endured into the twenty-first century—it can be found in the designs of many buildings and monuments, particularly in Washington, DC. The columns that support the two roofed entrances to the White House show a definite Roman influence. (This style of entrance is known as a portico—a word with Latin roots.) The Romans were fond of domed buildings—one of the most familiar landmarks in Washington is the dome of the US Capitol. Moreover, the front of the Capitol features arched entryways—another common feature of Roman architecture.

Roman culture is common in many other corners of modern society. Roman numerals are used in assorted documents—particularly on students' outlines. Roman numerals can also be found on the faces of many clocks, including the clocks found in the tower of Big Ben in London. Roman numerals can even be found on the trophy presented to the winner of the Super Bowl.

Even the calendar has a Roman influence—the months of July and August are, of course, named for Julius Caesar and Augustus. The names for the other months have Latin roots as well. Some are named for Roman gods: March is derived from Mars, the Roman god of war; June is named for Juno, goddess of women and childbirth; and January is named for Janus, the Roman god of gateways and beginnings. Most of the planets have also been named for Roman gods—Mercury, Venus, Mars, Jupiter, Saturn, Neptune, and Pluto.

The Julian calendar was adopted by Caesar for the empire in 46 BC It included 365 days divided into 12 months, with a leap day added every 4 years; therefore, the calendar averaged 365.25 days per year. The true year is actually about 11 minutes shorter than what the Julian calendar specified. Over the course of 4 centuries, these extra minutes added 3 days to the year—throwing everybody's calendars well off the mark of accuracy. In the sixteenth century Pope Gregory XIII adopted the Gregorian calendar, which corrects the problem by dropping 3 leap year days every 4 centuries. These days are dropped in the centennial years—for example, 1600 and 2000 were leap years, but 1700, 1800, and 1900 were not.

## Saga of Rome

The saga of ancient Rome has been told many times by writers and scholars in fiction and nonfiction, through books, plays, and films. Many high school English students will find themselves reading William Shakespeare's play *The Tragedy of Julius Caesar*, which has been performed many times onstage and adapted into cinematic versions.

The play tells the story of Caesar's assassination and the civil war that followed, culminating in the defeat of the conspirators by an army led by Octavius and Mark Antony at the Battle of Philippi. The play centers largely on the mental turmoil suffered by Caesar's closest friend, Marcus Junius Brutus, as he joins the conspiracy. As the assassins fall on Caesar and stab him with their daggers, Caesar sees his friend Brutus emerge from the mob and inflict the final wound. "*Et tu, Brute?*" Caesar asks as he succumbs to his wounds. The phrase translates to, "And you, Brutus?"

Shakespeare returned to ancient Rome to tell other stories. Among his other tragedies are *Coriolanus*, which tells the story of a conspiracy against one of Rome's first consuls; *Titus Andronicus*, a story of revenge involving a Roman general; and *Antony and Cleopatra*, which relates the story of Mark Antony and Cleopatra as they are pursued by Octavius.

Other writers have also reached into ancient Roman history. The Greek storyteller Aesop concocted the fable of Androcles, the slave

*American law, literature, and architecture reflect the influences of ancient Rome. One of the nation's most famous landmarks, the US Capitol Building in Washington, DC, features a dome and arched entryways—both commonly seen in Roman architecture.*

whose kindness to a lion was rewarded later when Androcles found himself facing the lion in an arena. The British playwright George Bernard Shaw took Aesop's fable and turned it into a comic play, titled *Androcles and the Lion*, about life in ancient Rome. In Shaw's version Androcles is a Christian slave who is to be fed to the lions in the Colosseum.

A much more serious story has been told by British author Robert Graves, whose novel *I, Claudius* covers the dark era of Roman history from the assassination of Julius Caesar to the death of Caligula. Required reading for serious students of ancient Rome is British author Edward Gibbon's *History of the Decline and Fall of the Roman Empire*. First published in 1776, unabridged versions of the huge work span eight volumes and more than 3,000 pages.

Hollywood has produced such classic films as *Cleopatra*, *Ben-Hur*, *The Last Days of Pompeii*, *Demetrius and the Gladiators*, *Quo Vadis*, *Spartacus*, and in more recent years, *Gladiator*, *Spartacus: Blood and Sand*, and *The Eagle*. Stage and film audiences have also enjoyed adaptations of the musical farce *A Funny Thing Happened on the Way to the Forum*, which is based on some of the slapstick comedies of the playwright Plautus.

The story of ancient Rome may have commenced when Aeneas sailed west to Rome from Troy about 3200 years ago or when two brothers, Romulus and Remus, fought to the death on a hilltop along the banks of the Tiber River about 2800 years ago. Or possibly Rome was founded by others, and their story has been lost in the depths of history. In the years following the city's founding, Rome produced the first truly representative government as well as powerful leaders who expanded their empire to its preeminent place on earth. Eventually, this most powerful of empires could not sustain itself. In the final analysis the most enduring legacy of ancient Rome may be the story of ancient Rome itself.

# Source Notes

## Introduction: The Defining Characteristics of Ancient Rome

1. Barry Cunliffe, *Rome and Her Empire*. New York: McGraw-Hill, 1978, p. 10.
2. Quoted in Charles R. Pellegrino, *Ghosts of Vesuvius: A New Look at the Last Days of Pompeii*. New York: HarperCollins, 2004, p. 308.
3. Cunliffe, *Rome and Her Empire*, p. 13.

## Chapter One: What Conditions Led to the Rise of Ancient Rome?

4. L.R. Lind, trans., *The Aeneid: An Epic Poem of Rome*. Bloomington: Indiana University Press, 1962, p. 3.
5. Cunliffe, *Rome and Her Empire*, p. 29.
6. Steven Bonta, "The Birth of the Republic," *New American*, October 4, 2004.
7. Quoted in Aubrey de Sélincourt, trans., *Livy: The Early History of Rome*. London: Penguin, 2002, p. 49.
8. Quoted in Cunliffe, *Rome and Her Empire*, p. 45.
9. Quoted in Cunliffe, *Rome and Her Empire*, p. 45.
10. Will Durant, *Caesar and Christ: The Story of Civilization III*. New York: Simon & Schuster, 1944, p. 15.
11. Quoted in Cunliffe, *Rome and Her Empire*, p. 46.
12. William Shakespeare, *Shakespeare's Rape of Lucrece*. London: Aldine House, 1896, p. 92.
13. Livy, *The History of Rome*, vol. 1. Whitefish, MT: Kessinger, 2004, p. 66.
14. Steven Bonta, "The Republic Matures," *New American*, October 18, 2004, p. 35.

## Chapter Two: Wars of Expansion

15. Durant, *Caesar and Christ*, p. 410.

16. Quoted in Alfred John Church, *Stories from Livy*. New York: Dodd, Mead, 1883, pp. 187–88.

17. Quoted in Colleen McCullough, *The First Man in Rome*. New York: Avon, 2008, p. 994.

18. Durant, *Caesar and Christ*, p. 119.

19. Quoted in John J. McGrath, ed., *An Army at War: Change in the Midst of Conflict*. Fort Leavenworth, KS: Combat Studies Institute, 2005, p. 152.

20. Durant, *Caesar and Christ*, pp. 40–41.

21. Cunliffe, *Rome and Her Empire*, pp. 68–69.

22. Cunliffe, *Rome and Her Empire*, p. 71.

23. Quoted in Adrian Keith Goldsworthy, *Caesar: Life of a Colossus*. New Haven, CT: Yale University, 2006, p. 447.

## Chapter Three: The Roman Empire at Its Height

24. J.P.V.D. Balsdon, *Life and Leisure in Ancient Rome*. London: Phoenix, 2002, pp. 259–60.

25. Durant, *Caesar and Christ*, p. 361.

26. Durant, *Caesar and Christ*, p. 134.

27. Balsdon, *Life and Leisure in Ancient Rome*, p. 288.

28. Cunliffe, *Rome and Her Empire*, p. 13.

29. Balsdon, *Life and Leisure in Ancient Rome*, p. 28.

30. Durant, *Caesar and Christ*, p. 289.

31. Durant, *Caesar and Christ*, p. 289.

32. Durant, *Caesar and Christ*, p. 138.

## Chapter 4: Rome's Slow Decline

33. Milton S. Terry, trans., *The Sibylline Oracles*. New York: Hunt & Eaton, 1890, p. 176.

34. Quoted in Matthew Gelzer, *Caesar: Politician and Statesman*. Cambridge, MA: Harvard University Press, 1997, p. 327.

35. E.O. Windstedt, trans., *Cicero: Letters to Atticus*, vol. 2. New York: MacMillan, 1913, pp. 161–63.

36. Quoted in Chris Scarre, *Chronicle of the Roman Emperors*. London: Thames & Hudson, 1995, p. 29.

37. Quoted in Scarre, *Chronicle of the Roman Emperors*, p. 29.

38. Durant, *Caesar and Christ*, p. 263.

39. Quoted in Scarre, *Chronicle of the Roman Emperors*, p. 57.

40. Quoted in Kathryn Welch, *The Romans*. New York: Rizzoli, 1998, p. 134.

41. Quoted in Brian W. Jones, *The Emperor Domitian*. New York: Routledge, 1992, p. 116.

42. Robert Louis Wilken, *The Spirit of Early Christian Thought: Seeking the Face of God*. New Haven, CT: Yale University Press, 2003, p. 224.

43. Durant, *Caesar and Christ*, p. 629.

## Chapter 5: What Is the Legacy of Ancient Rome?

44. Steven Bonta, "Lessons of Rome," *New American*, February 21, 2005, p. 36.

45. Bonta, "Lessons of Rome," p. 36.

46. Quoted in Jeffrey H. Morrison, *The Political Philosophy of George Washington*. Baltimore: Johns Hopkins University Press, 2009, p. 84.

47. Quoted in Morrison, *The Political Philosophy of George Washington*, p. 85.

48. Michael Grant, *The Collapse and Recovery of the Roman Empire*. New York: Routledge, 2000, p. 79.

49. Quoted in Alexander Scobie, *Hitler's State Architecture: The Impact of Classical Antiquity*. University Park: Pennsylvania State University Press, 1990, p. 9.

# Important People of Ancient Rome

**Augustus:** Born Gaius Octavius, he was the adopted son of Julius Caesar. When Caesar was assassinated, Octavius returned to Rome and joined forces with Caesar's ally, Mark Antony, to hunt down the conspirators. Octavius emerged from the civil war as Rome's first emperor. Under Augustus, the Senate and People's Assembly became virtually powerless.

**Julius Caesar:** The Roman general returned to Rome after a successful campaign against the Gauls. When the Senate ordered Caesar to disband his army, he refused and instead marched on Rome. The Senate quickly conferred on Caesar the title of dictator. He used his authority to hunt down his enemies, sparking a civil war. In 44 BC, fearing that Caesar had grown too powerful, a group of patricians assassinated the dictator.

**Marcus Tullius Cicero:** A statesman, philosopher, orator, consul, and member of the Senate, Cicero spoke out against the disintegration of the Roman republic under Julius Caesar. Despite his eloquent pleas to be wary of Caesar, the Senate ignored him and made Caesar dictator for life. After Caesar's assassination, Cicero spoke out against Mark Antony, who had assumed absolute authority. To silence Cicero, Antony had him murdered.

**Lucius Quinctius Cincinnatus:** Cincinnatus led Rome during one of its first crises—an attack by a neighboring tribe. The Senate gave him complete authority. When the crisis passed, Cincinnatus gave up his power and returned to his farm. The American Founding Fathers hoped the leaders of their new nation would serve as Cincinnatus had served—as patriots who would answer the call to duty, then humbly return to their private lives.

**Diocletian:** By the time Diocletian became emperor of Rome in AD 284, the empire was under siege by its enemies and suffering from internal strife. To ease tensions, Diocletian split the empire into four sections, appointing caesars to rule over each region. Diocletian also moved the capital to a city in Turkey. Diocletian's reforms helped stabilize the empire only temporarily. Meanwhile, he stepped up persecution of the Christians.

**Hannibal:** The leader of the Carthaginian army crossed the Mediterranean Sea and led his troops toward Rome, sparking the Second Punic War. Hannibal's army appeared ready to advance on Rome, but he inexplicably stalled the advance. His error in strategy provided the Romans the opportunity to march toward Carthage, which eventually resulted in the defeat of Hannibal and the end of Carthage as a state.

**Titus Livius:** Known as Livy, he was a writer and historian who obliged Emperor Augustus by producing a lengthy history of Rome, concentrating on the triumphs of Rome's heroes. Livy's *History of Rome from Its Foundation* contain a number of historical inaccuracies, but his prose is widely praised for bringing drama and a human voice to ancient Rome's long history.

**Nero:** The Roman emperor ordered the murder of his mother and horrified the aristocracy by fancying himself an actor. He initiated a long era of persecution against the Christians by having them arrested, tortured, and killed in the Roman arenas. Nero committed suicide in AD 68 after the Roman Senate, believing him to be insane, ordered his arrest and execution.

**Romulus:** Romulus is believed to have been the founder of the city of Rome in 753 BC. According to legend, Romulus and his brother Remus were abandoned as babies and raised by a she-wolf. As teenagers the brothers led their followers to a bend in the Tiber River. When priests declared Romulus king, Remus refused to accept the judgment and fought his brother. Romulus prevailed and reigned over Rome for 36 years.

**Spartacus:** A slave and gladiator trainee from Thrace, Spartacus led a slave revolt that eventually drew some 250,000 followers. The slaves won several encounters with the Roman army, but in 71 BC the decisive battle was fought at Reggio Calabria, a city on the southern tip of the Italian Peninsula. Spartacus was killed in battle, and some 6,000 slaves captured by the Roman army were crucified.

**Tarquinius Superbus:** The last of the Etruscan kings, Tarquinius's despotism helped spark the rebellion that led to his ouster and the establishment of the Roman republic. Tarquinius assassinated his democracy-minded brother-in-law, then ruled Rome with an iron fist for 25 years. When Tarquinius's son raped the wife of a Roman aristocrat, Romans rose up in rebellion.

**Publius Valerius:** One of the first consuls of the Roman republic, Publius drafted some of Rome's earliest laws. Known as Publicola, or the "friend of the people," Publius wrote laws establishing the death penalty for anybody who declared himself king of Rome. He also lowered taxes for poor people and granted the right of appeal to condemned prisoners.

# For Further Research

## Books

Mary Beard, *The Fires of Vesuvius: Pompeii Lost and Found*. Cambridge, MA: Harvard University Press, 2010.

Stephen Dando-Collins, *The Great Fire of Rome: The Fall of the Emperor Nero and His City*. Cambridge, MA: Da Capo, 2010.

———, *Legions of Rome*. London: Quercus, 2010.

Phillip Freeman, *Julius Caesar*. New York: Simon & Schuster, 2009.

Peter J. Leithart, *Defending Constantine: The Twilight of an Empire and the Dawn of Christendom*. Downers Grove, IL: InterVarsity, 2010.

Philip Matyszak, *Chronicle of the Roman Republic: The Rulers of Ancient Rome from Romulus to Augustus*. New York: Thames & Hudson, 2008.

Konstantin Nossov, *Gladiator: Rome's Bloody Spectacle*. Oxford: Osprey, 2009.

Stacy Schiff, *Cleopatra: A Life*. New York: Little, Brown, 2010.

Barry Strauss, *The Spartacus War*. New York: Simon & Schuster, 2009.

Katherine E. Welch, *The Roman Amphitheatre: From Its Origins to the Colosseum*. New York: Cambridge University Press, 2009.

## Websites

**Encyclopedia Romana** (http://penelope.uchicago.edu/~grout/encyclopaedia_romana). Maintained by the University of Chicago, the online encyclopedia covers many topics of interest to students of ancient Rome. In addition to descriptions of historical events and biographies of important figures in Roman history, the archive contains many maps, photos, and other images depicting life in ancient Rome.

**National Junior Classical League** (www.njcl.org). The organization of 50,000 Latin students includes more than 1,200 local chapters, mostly Latin clubs sponsored by American high schools. Visitors to the website will find information on joining as well as the league's activities, including the availability of scholarships and the annual conventions held at American universities.

**The Punic Wars** (www.boisestate.edu/courses/westciv/punicwar). Maintained by Boise State University, the Internet site provides an overview of the three Punic Wars. Visitors can find descriptions of the battles, maps, biographies of Hannibal and Scipio, and an overview of the political situation that led to the hostilities between Rome and Carthage.

**"Roman Bath,"** *Secrets of Lost Empires* (www.pbs.org/wgbh/nova/lostempires/roman). Companion website to the episode in the PBS *Nova* series *Secrets of Lost Empires* that explored the Roman baths. Visitors can find information on the aqueducts that fed water to the city and explore architectural drawings and other images of typical baths used by Romans during the ancient era.

*The Roman Empire in the First Century* (www.pbs.org/empires/romans/index.html). The companion website to the PBS documentary series *The Roman Empire in the First Century* offers many resources for students, including a timeline, excerpts from the writings of Roman authors, a family tree of Emperor Augustus, and an overview of gladiatorial combat, Roman baths, and pagan religious rites.

*The Sibylline Oracles* (www.sacred-texts.com/cla/sib/index.htm). A translation of *The Sibylline Oracles* can be found on this website. In addition to the translation, students can find abundant footnotes explaining the text and interpreting the prophecies. An index providing the names of many noted personalities of ancient Rome is also included.

*The Strategemata* (http://penelope.uchicago.edu/Thayer/E/Roman/Texts/Frontinus/Strategemata/home.html). For students who want to explore the strategies employed by the Roman army, the University of Chicago has made a translation of *The Strategemata* by Sextus Julius Frontinus available at this website. The author covers such strategies as surprise attacks, inducing treachery in the ranks of the enemy, and terrorizing the army's besieged foes.

**Titus Livius: The History of Rome** (http://etext.virginia.edu/toc/modeng/public/Liv1His.html). The University of Virginia Library has made Livy's *History of Rome from Its Foundation* available on this website. Students can read Roman history in Livy's own words.

# Index

Note: Boldface page numbers indicate illustrations.

# Picture Credits

# About the Author

Hal Marcovitz is a former newspaper reporter and columnist and the author of more than 150 books for young readers. He is coauthor of *Bloom's Literary Places: Rome*, a guide to the landmarks in Rome that have served as inspiration to writers. He makes his home in Chalfont, Pennsylvania, with his wife, Gail, and daughter Ashley.